W9-CFZ-124

The Future of Information Services

The Future of Information Services

Virginia Steel
C. Brigid Welch
Editors

The Haworth Press, Inc.
New York · London

The Future of Information Services has also been published as *Journal of Library Administration*, Volume 20, Numbers 3/4 1995.

The Haworth Press, Inc., 10 Alice Street, Binghamton, NY 13904-1580

Library of Congress Cataloging-in-Publication Data

The future of information services / Virginia Steel, C. Brigid Welch.
     p.   cm.
    "Has also been published as Journal of library administration, vol. 20, numbers 3/4 1995"–T.p. verso.
    Includes bibliographical references.
    ISBN 1-56024-738-X (alk. paper)
    1. Libraries–United States–Data processing. 2. Library information networks–United States. 3. Information networks–United States. 4. Information services–United States–Data processing. I. Steel, Virginia. II. Welch, C. Brigid.
Z678.9.A4U634 1995
025'.00285–dc20
                                            95-1692
                                            CIP

INDEXING & ABSTRACTING

Contributions to this publication are selectively indexed or abstracted in print, electronic, online, or CD-ROM version(s) of the reference tools and information services listed below. This list is current as of the copyright date of this publication. See the end of this section for additional notes.

- *Academic Abstracts/CD-ROM,* EBSCO Publishing, P.O. Box 2250, Peabody, MA 01960-7250

- *AGRICOLA Database,* National Agricultural Library, 10301 Baltimore Boulevard, Room 002, Beltsville, MD 20705

- *Cambridge Scientific Abstracts, Health & Safety Science Abstracts,* Cambridge Information Group, 7200 Wisconsin Avenue #601, Bethesda, MD 20814

- *Current Articles on Library Literature and Services (CALLS),* Pakistan Library Association, Quaid-e-Azam Library, Bagh-e-Jinnah, Lahore, Pakistan

- *Current Awareness Bulletin,* Association for Information Management, Information House, 20-24 Old Street, London EC1V 9AP, England

- *Current Index to Journals in Education,* Syracuse University, 4-194 Center for Science and Technology, Syracuse, NY 13244-4100

- *Educational Administration Abstracts (EAA),* Sage Publications, Inc., 2455 Teller Road, Newbury Park, CA 91320

- *Higher Education Abstracts,* Claremont Graduate School, 740 North College Avenue, Claremont, CA 91711

- *Index to Periodical Articles Related to Law,* University of Texas, 727 East 26th Street, Austin, TX 78705

- *Information Reports & Bibliographies,* Science Associates International, Inc., 465 West End Avenue, New York, NY 10024

- *Information Science Abstracts,* Plenum Publishing Company, 233 Spring Street, New York, NY 10013-1578

- *Informed Librarian, The,* Infosources Publishing, 140 Norma Road, Teaneck, NJ 07666

(continued)

- *INSPEC Information Services,* Institution of Electrical Engineers, Michael Faraday House, Six Hills Way, Stevenage, Herts SG1 2AY, England
- *INTERNET ACCESS (& additional networks) Bulletin Board for Libraries ("BUBL"), coverage of information resources on INTERNET, JANET, and other networks.*
  - JANET X.29: UK.AC.BATH.BUBL or 00006012101300
  - TELNET: BUBL.BATH.AC.UK or 138.38.32.45 login 'bubl'
  - GOPHER: BUBL.BATH.AC.UK (138.32.32.45). Port 7070
  - World Wide Web: http: / / www.bubl.bath.ac.uk./BUBL/home.html
  - NISSWAIS: Telnetniss.ac.uk (for the NISS gateway)
  The Andersonian Library, Curran Building, 101 St. James Road, Glasgow G4 ONS, Scotland
- *Library & Information Science Abstracts (LISA),* Bowker-Saur Limited, Maypole House, Maypole Road, East Grinstead, West Sussex RH19 1HH, England
- *Library Literature,* The H.W. Wilson Company, 950 University Avenue, Bronx, NY 10452
- *Newsletter of Library and Information Services,* China Sci-Tech Book Review, Library of Academia Sinica, 8 Kexueyuan Nanlu, Zhongguancun, Beijing 10080 People Republic of China
- *OT BibSys,* American Occupational Therapy Foundation, P.O. Box 1725, Rockville, MD 20849-1725
- *PASCAL International Bibliography T205: Sciences de l'information Documentation,* INIST/CNRS–Service Gestion des Documents Primaries, 2, Allee du Parc de Brabois, F-54514 Vandoeuvre-les-Nancy, Cedex France
- *Public Affairs Information Bulletin (PAIS),* Public Affairs Information Service, Inc., 521 West 43rd Street, New York, NY 10036-4396
- *Referativnyi Zhurnal (Abstracts Journal of the Institute of Scientific Information of the Republic of Russia),* The Institute of Scientific Information, Baltijskaja ul., 14, Moscow A-219, Republic of Russia
- *Trade & Industry Index,* Information Access Company, 362 Lakeside Drive, Foster City, CA 94404
- *Women in Management Review Abstract,* Anbar Abstracts, 62 Toller Lane, Bradford, West Yorkshire BD8 9BY, England

Book reviews are selectively excerpted by the *Guide to Professional Literature of the Journal of Academic Librarianship.*

The Future of Information Services

CONTENTS

∞ ALL HAWORTH BOOKS AND JOURNALS
   ARE PRINTED ON CERTIFIED
   ACID-FREE PAPER

ABOUT THE EDITORS

Virginia Steel is Head of the Social Sciences and Humanities Library at the University of California, San Diego. She received her BA from University of Rochester in foreign literature and an MA from the Graduate Library School, University of Chicago. She has held public services and administrative positions at the Arizona State University Libraries, and in 1990 was selected as a Council on Library Resources Management Intern, serving at Brown University.

C. Brigid Welch is currently Acting Head of Document Delivery Services, Gelman Library, The George Washington University, where she manages the operations of the Interlibrary Loan and Borrowing Programs and the Gelman Library Information Service. She has a BA in English Literature from Arizona State University and an MLS from The University of Texas at Austin. She has held public services and management positions at the University of Houston Libraries and the University of California at San Diego Libraries. She has worked for ALA's Association of College and Research Libraries as Program Officer for Bibliographic Instruction and Continuing Education and as Assistant Editor at *Choice Magazine*. As Senior Program Officer for Information Services at the Office of Management Services (OMS), Association of Research Libraries, 1990/94, Welch was editor and publisher of OMS Publications including the SPEC Kit series.

Introduction

The rapid proliferation of technology to create, store, retrieve, and disseminate information has resulted in the now-cliched Information Explosion. Aided and abetted by technology, information is being produced at the fastest rate in human history. Information has become a valuable commodity, leading to a shift from a manufacturing-based to an information-based economy–an economy which itself has undergone a major paradigm shift from a national, or multinational, economy to a global economy.

Against this dynamic backdrop, library users are changing their expectations and demands for services; computers and telecommunications technology are redefining the library's structure and services; and information is being made available in a multiplicity of formats. Compounding these challenges is a fundamental scarcity of resources brought about by a shrinking U.S. economy and declining revenues.

In the context of emerging technologies and changing user needs, many academic and public libraries are engaged in intensive self-examination and strategic planning. In addition to day-to-day operations, library administrators and staff are investing a tremendous amount of time and energy in a variety of activities designed to meet the challenges libraries are facing, including: assessing user needs and services performance; examining organizational, staffing, and management of services; planning for and using new technology; identifying viable partnerships, both with vendors and clients; and articulating and implementing information services programs. Early results of these strategic activities are demonstrating

[Haworth co-indexing entry note]: "Introduction." Steel, Virginia, and C. Brigid Welch. Co-published simultaneously in *Journal of Library Administration* (The Haworth Press, Inc.) Vol. 20, Nos. 3/4, 1995, pp. 1-8; and: *The Future of Information Services* (ed: Virginia Steel, and C. Brigid Welch) The Haworth Press, Inc., 1995, pp. 1-8. Multiple copies of this article/chapter may be purchased from The Haworth Document Delivery Center [1-800-3-HAWORTH; 9:00 a.m. - 5:00 p.m. (EST)].

as great a spirit of risk-taking and as high a degree of innovation as libraries have ever experienced.

Libraries cannot escape the changes this dynamic information environment is bringing about–nor do they want to. Yet the unrelenting pressure to get on the information superhighway, the need to re-engineer traditional library organizations, and the slashing of library budgets have made it increasingly difficult for librarians and administrators to know what the range of services and organizational structures will be next year, let alone in 5 or 10 years. Even so, it is imperative that librarians and library administrators consider the future of information services and delivery if they wish to be successful in surviving as vital organizations and if they want to influence the direction libraries will head in the future.

The focus of this volume is on the long-range outlook for libraries, and it includes discussion of the implications for organizational structures and services. The contributors share their thoughts on many of the issues that need to be resolved in order for libraries to survive and flourish in the 21st century.

The initial topic is organizational development and administration. One of the most important elements needed to guide library organizations as they evolve is administrative leadership skills. Merrily E. Taylor offers an insightful analysis of the environment in which libraries find themselves, the leadership skills and qualities that have been prevalent in the past, and the new talents and abilities that are necessary to realize the library of the next century. She points out that libraries as organizations are widely perceived as static, independent organizations that operate autonomously; as library administrators and librarians well know, this perception is not accurate. To provide the vision and leadership essential to bring about organizational change and to be successful as advocates for support for libraries, Ms. Taylor makes a strong case that administrators must possess political acumen, patience, flexibility, a high degree of tolerance for ambiguity, the ability to communicate and to create a sense of teamwork within libraries and with other entities outside libraries, and a courageous nature that is willing to take risks as libraries evolve.

The second paper moves beyond the leadership skills needed to discuss the types of organizational issues that must be grappled with and resolved to make libraries more responsive to the environment in which they find themselves. Carolyn Gray reviews several of the management theories that have guided library organizational development in past decades and then goes on to recommend a model for the future that calls for integration of information services staff with systems staff. The advantages of this model are many, but one of the most significant is the cross-training that happens when systems staff work closely with public services librarians; this sharing of technical knowledge is critical as library services continue to increase their reliance on technology to identify and deliver information.

The changing environment of electronic resources and the emerging information superhighway are widely reported in the media and widely discussed topics at professional meetings. The Clinton Administration support for the National Information Infrastructure has only hastened the inevitable progress toward linked information systems that provide access to users around the globe, thus increasing the pressure on libraries to provide access to these resources. In their article Kenneth H. Dowlin and Katherine N. Wingerson present a new model for the public library, a model that focuses on networked access, differentiated levels of service, and direct delivery. The authors argue that the public library must be a partner in the building of a local information infrastructure, and they outline the steps the San Francisco Public Library is taking toward building such a Community Electronic Information Infrastructure (CEII).

Following on the discussion of leadership skills, the next articles review the major functions and departments included in most academic and public libraries to see what significant differences there may be in the library of the future. Margaret Morrison examines the changes that are likely to occur in reference services, including new structures, different individual responsibilities for librarians and paraprofessionals, and the constant introduction of new technologies. The message delivered by Ms. Morrison reinforces the concept of the user as the central focus around which reference and other library services are developed.

In an article about the future of bibliographic instruction, Carolyn Dusenbury and Barbara Pease continue exploring the evolution in library instructional programs that may well occur as educational and information-seeking models change. There is a plethora of resources available to help users find information, and new databases and electronic services are appearing daily. Finding relevant information to answer a specific need can be a complex undertaking if systems do not have uniform interfaces designed in a way that enables users to navigate them easily and intuitively. Librarians and administrators must add their voices to those of the mass of users in order to influence the design of future systems. What must be brought together is an amalgam that incorporates video, text, and data using the most advanced tools available: this will be the critical tool of the 21st century. By virtue of their involvement in instructional activities, public services librarians are well-situated to make useful contributions to the development of new and improved library programs.

Just as reference and instructional services are evolving, the future of government documents collections and services is equally uncertain. Linda Kennedy offers an overview of recent developments that will undoubtedly affect the future of the U.S. public documents program, including highlights of the major initiatives, such as the National Information Infrastructure (NII), undertaken by the Clinton Administration. When one considers the growth in privatization of government programs, the move to electronic media to disseminate government information, and the NII, it is clear that these will all have a significant impact on the ability of depository libraries to continue to provide the level and amount of service that has been offered in the past.

Going beyond the boundaries of the United States, Paul Zarins takes a look at the international information arena. He points out that we now find ourselves living in a global community with the need to have ready access to information from countries around the globe. Unfortunately, many barriers exist that complicate access to international information; if libraries are to be successful in meeting the needs of their users, they must confront the problems associated with identification and retrieval of materials from other countries and from international organizations.

Just as international information can be difficult to locate and obtain, materials in many libraries' Special Collections operations remain uncataloged and unused. Stanley Chodorow and Lynda Corey Claassen explore the problems associated with the traditional academic library Special Collections departments that have resulted in low-use, expensive treasure houses that do not bear any relation to academic programs. They propose a change in outlook for Special Collections administrators and librarians to make the collections more relevant to local research and teaching and to draw faculty and students into the library to use these materials. Technology is not to be overlooked as a tool that can enhance access to Special Collections materials, and the authors suggest that it might well be the means by which rare and fragile materials could be shared widely. In order to survive and grow, Special Collections administrators must make careful choices as they structure their collections and services; otherwise they run the risk of having their budgets and operations cut or eliminated as libraries try to cope with decreasing financial resources.

As a way of dealing with the dire fiscal situation in which libraries currently exist, Stephen Coffman discusses the value and opportunities available if libraries move in the direction of providing services and resources for a fee. As he points out, the environment in which libraries operate currently is bleak: budgets are being slashed, library schools are closing, and there is increasing competition for libraries as the commercial sector begins to recognize the profit potential of the information superhighway. Currently over 400 public, academic, and special libraries operate fee-based information services on a cost-recovery basis. These client-centered services offer customized research and document delivery services for a fee to the individual library's user population: chief among their clients are the library's non-primary users, typically from the business, professional, and media sectors, as well as independent researchers.

The number of fee-based services in public and academic libraries is growing, and Coffman argues that these types of services for a fee offer libraries different revenue sources that would allow continued delivery of information services and materials to customers who request them. The underlying philosophy of equal access to libraries and the information made available through them would have to change if libraries universally move in this direction, but this article makes the case that offering enhanced services to those clientele requesting (and willing to pay for) such information services may be the only way for public libraries to survive and provide basic services free to users.

John Haak, Helen B. Josephine, and Glenn Miyataki take the discussion of fee-based services further in their article that describes the vision and planning that have gone into creation of a partnership between the state of Hawai'i and the University of Hawai'i Library. Their joint venture is an effort to provide information services from the rich resources of the rapidly expanding Pacific Rim region to the community as a way of fostering economic growth and development.

Another issue is the exploration of partnerships in the information future. It includes two articles that examine other relationships that have a strong impact on the future of information services. The first is a discussion of library and information studies education by Jeffrey T. Huber. As he points out, the past years have witnessed an increasing tension between library schools that teach theoretical models of the profession and library managers who wish to find specific competencies already mastered by new librarians they hire. Given the technological changes that are occurring so rapidly, this article suggests that library schools can redefine their curricula to teach students the underlying concepts of information identification and retrieval and to prepare them for a profession that will undergo tremendous change throughout their careers.

The last article in this volume concerns the relationship between libraries and the automation vendors that serve them. George R. Plosker and Linnea J. Christiani review the key questions that library administrators must ask when working with vendors, and they recognize that librarians and vendors must work together to provide access to the information that will be demanded by users. If vendors resist change, they run the same risks that libraries do of becoming obsolete or being forced out of business. The advent of technology has made libraries and vendors dependent on one another for continued survival.

Libraries as organizations are undergoing a metamorphosis into libraries of the 21st century–libraries that will offer easy access to the vast information resources of the world. At times, the challenge to create and implement information services and programs for our clients seems no less than creating information order out of information chaos.

While various visions about the information services future are presented by each of the contributors to this volume, one common thread runs through each offering–the library user must be the major partner in planning for the future of information services. While we may only imagine much of what the future holds, the reality is that library users must play an equal role with librarians in the definition and implementation of the services. Librarians must continue to value user feedback about information needs, information-seeking behavior, and the degree of success they have when using libraries. This feedback is even more critical now than ever before.

Librarians are in a unique position to provide leadership as society works toward the information future. Successful leadership during these seemingly chaotic times will require a high degree of creativity, risk-taking, and innovation. It will also require a clear understanding and articulation of our professional values and vision. Margaret Wheatley in her book, *Leadership and the New Science: Learning about Organization from an Orderly Universe,* argues that leadership of today's organizations requires a grounding of our work as members of the organization in the principles of the "new science," that is " . . . the revolutionary discoveries in quantum physics, class theory, and molecular biology that are changing our understanding of the universe."[1]

In searching for answers in such a dynamic atmosphere, Wheatley suggests that "the motion of these systems is kept in harmony by a force we are just beginning to appreciate: the capacity for self-reference."[2] Each part of the system remains consistent with itself, its essence, and with all other parts of the system as it changes.[3] Librarians must understand, appreciate, and trust our essence–our values as professionals and our vision of the future–in order to use the power of self-reference as we form the partnerships and engage in the dialogue necessary to shape the future of information services.

Virginia Steel
C. Brigid Welch

NOTES

1. Margaret Wheatley, *Leadership and the New Science: Learning about Organization from an Orderly Universe* (San Francisco: Berrett-Koehler Publishers, 1992), 144.

2. Wheatley, p. 146.

3. Wheatley, p. 147.

Getting It All Together:
Leadership Requirements for the Future
of Information Services

Merrily E. Taylor

On May 18, 1993, *The New York Times Magazine* offered a cover story entitled, "The Telephone Transformed–Into Almost Everything."[1] The article, by James Gleick, made the case that as the result of a convergence of technologies hitherto independent (telephones, television, computers, and fax machines, to name several), we are about to undergo "social changes so profound (that) their only parallel is probably the discovery of fire." Gleick asks the question, "Is this technology about to liberate us or to overwhelm us?"[2]

Librarians, of course, have seen this question on the horizon for a number of years and have been aware of both the promise, and the perils, of The Information Age. We know that, increasingly, information will no longer be hostage to time, format, or place, and that it will be both more voluminous and more available to the end user. We know that the Library as we have known it will be transformed, although we are not yet sure as to what form this transformation will take. We know that librarians are daily being required to develop new skills, and that even the term "librarian" may someday

---

Merrily E. Taylor is University Librarian at Brown University, Providence, RI.

[Haworth co-indexing entry note]: "Getting It All Together: Leadership Requirements for the Future of Information Services." Taylor, Merrily E. Co-published simultaneously in *Journal of Library Administration* (The Haworth Press, Inc.) Vol. 20, Nos. 3/4, 1995, pp. 9-24; and: *The Future of Information Services* (ed: Virginia Steel, and C. Brigid Welch) The Haworth Press, Inc., 1995, pp. 9-24. Multiple copies of this article/chapter may be purchased from The Haworth Document Delivery Center [1-800-3-HAWORTH; 9:00 a.m. - 5:00 p.m. (EST)].

come to connote someone quite different from the model of the last several centuries. We know that many of the traditional mechanisms established to guide users through an already complex information universe will require "translation" for the 21st Century library, dependent as contemporary users are on limited, rigid indexing systems and the necessity to "go to the reference desk." We know that popular entertainment media of all kinds will make good use of the Information Highway; we are less sure about how scholarly information will make the transition.

What seems certain, amongst a plethora of glittering and sometimes scary possibilities, is that beginning and mid-career librarians are about to embark on a journey of discovery to an information services future which we can only partly envision. What leadership qualities should we seek in the library directors who will help guide our institutions toward that future, and who may find themselves managing 21st Century information services? What leadership qualities should library directors attempt to develop and nurture amongst their staffs? The case can be made that new or different leadership qualities may not be required at all; what will be required for information services leadership in the future is a generous helping of the same characteristics which have typically been found in the successful leaders of large, complex, and volatile enterprises. The *difference* may be that we have come to realize, perhaps belatedly, that libraries fall logically within this category.

Rightly or wrongly, in many quarters libraries are still seen as stable, conservative, simple places which have changed little over the centuries and which are primarily the repository of the book. While it is acknowledged (by the few people outside libraries who have thought about it) that libraries are complicated organizations, and share much in common with any organization of a certain size and structure, libraries are defined in the public mind most commonly in terms of a *structure* and an *object*–a building full of books. To generalize, one could say that "the man or woman on the street" is confident that s/he knows what the library *is,* and what it *does.* Because the outward appearance of the library seems so understandable and unchanging, libraries are perceived as threatened when place and format are no longer relevant ("the library without walls"), when the library's supposed agenda (getting more and more books) is called into question, or when there is ambiguity about where a particular "library" service may belong functionally (hence the not infrequent tension among libraries, computer centers, media services departments, etc.).

In keeping with this traditional view, we tend to think of library directors as those who have the primary responsibility for a specific building or set of buildings constituting the "library," or for an organization which carries out a series of library functions as presently defined. What is too little recognized, discussed or analyzed is the fundamental societal purpose represented by the institution we have traditionally called a "library," a purpose which is independent of the library building or organization as such. It is even independent, as past decades have demonstrated, of the book. If we keep in mind this fundamental societal purpose, we may then see directors as those who are charged with conceptualizing, managing, articulating, and preserving something which Oscar Handlin, former Harvard University Librarian, once referred to as *The Idea of a Library*. Here, much edited, is how Handlin distinguished "the idea" of a library from the image of a "warehouse full of books":

> If we look at the purpose of the library in the lives of those who use it, we will see that it is not just a book warehouse, it is not just a museum. It is a collection of a series of collections which have a purpose and a direct relationship to the life of the community in which the library develops . . . the collection has constantly to be developed in light of the purpose it serves . . . developing a collection . . . means not simply adding to it but also subtracting from it and providing the kind of judgments that would apply the preservation process not simply to keeping what is there intact but to improving what is there for the purpose of its future users . . . The library does not serve only its present users. The library is here. It was here 20, 30 years ago—in Harvard's case 300 years ago—and it will be here for a long time after the current crop of users shuffles on its way. And that subtly alters the purpose of the library and reshapes the character of its mission . . . the librarian has a kind of heritage. He does not walk among blank shelves.[3]

The library, in other words, is not simply a building full of books or an organization in the political sense. Neither is it a "network full of databases," however extensive or impressive. A "library" is a series of related collections, developed in conscious acknowledgment of the community to be served, and preserved and shaped over time for use not only by the present generation, but by generations to come. It is a series of collections which are organized in such a fashion as to facilitate use, and which moreover are served by staff who are capable of building and structuring the collections and of assisting users who require help. As an enterprise, the library represents the societal values of amassing and preserving information of significance to the community and to the history of humankind; organizing that information in such a way as to transform it into knowledge; and actively taking steps to encourage use. A further value, at least in a democratic society, is that access to that information be free or at least provided on some equitable basis to all who need it. An enterprise which in some characteristics *resembles* a library, but which lacks the bulk of the aforesaid qualities, is not a library in any true sense of the word. Handlin recognized this when he described his visit to several great "libraries" in the former East Germany: " . . . I had the opportunity to visit the library of the ancient, respected University in Leipzig . . . I mucked around in the catalogs to see what this collection amounted to, and I discovered to my distress that no doubt there were three million volumes there but that a student interested in . . . Modern History could not get any of the materials available to scholars of the same period in most libraries of the West . . . thousands of students in the University of Leipzig did not have a library in the sense that we understand it."[4]

At the moment, the prodigious and disorganized digital information available to us through the Internet shares only fragments of the values which define the library, and thus cannot truly represent one, however enthusiastically we may prophesy about "digital libraries" and "the library without walls." This situation does not need to remain the case, however. The task of library leaders, both of today and tomorrow, is to preserve and carry forward the *idea* of the library in an age when information is not hostage to format, time, or space and when "library" cannot easily be defined as a building full of books or even as an organization providing certain well-established functions. Tomorrow's library—indeed, today's—is thus a large, complex and volatile undertaking, no place for the rigid, the timid, the unimaginative, or the unadventurous. Robin Alston, of University College, London, made this point in a lecture on February 16, 1993, when he said,

> the survival of the institutions we call libraries will depend, as always, on enlightened and imaginative librarians able to develop within a hostile political environment a model which can adapt to the evolving need of research in all disciplines. Those needs will, within a decade, include access to information in a wide variety of databases, electronic archives of images and sounds, as well as the cultural inheritance in print and manuscript . . . one consequence of this is the self-evident need for librarians in the future to develop both ancient and modern skills. The notion that knowledge can prosper by creating vast knowledge warehouses based on the hypermarket model—you can buy it if you can find it—is sheer fantasy . . .[5]

What, then, characterizes the successful leaders of large, volatile and complex enterprises? It is clear that one of the primary characteristics of such leaders is an ability to lead in a climate of ambiguity, and to live in a world where there are few easy answers. Harlan Cleveland, management expert and former President of the University of Hawaii, characterizes administration as the "get-it-all-together profession," and administrators as those who are able to bring many varied, discordant elements together in order to get something accomplished.[6] In his book *The Knowledge Executive: Leadership in an Information Society* (N. Y., E. P. Dutton, 1985), Cleveland makes the point that, in an increasingly complex age, " . . . the art of executive leadership is above all a taste for paradox, a talent for ambiguity, the capacity to hold contradictory propositions comfortably in a mind that relishes complexity. The executive function is to bring people together in organizations to make something different happen."[7]

Today's information world is a world of paradox and contradiction. It is easier and easier to distribute and reproduce information, and we are more concerned than ever about copyright and intellectual property. More information surrounds us than ever before, and (because of both cost and our inability to deal with volume) we have less and less of it accessible to us. Information technology enthusiasts predict that soon the easy availability of electronic information to end users will make libraries, and librarians, obsolete, at the same time that many of us sense a greater, not lesser, need for trained information professionals. Technology, oblivious to time and distance, will bring us together; technology, if not made reasonably available to all, will tear us apart. The book is outmoded; the book is about to become more precious than ever, because its more mundane uses will be the province of technology, and only the most significant information will make it into print. We have more technologies than ever for the preservation of information printed on acidic paper, but we are worried about the "shelf-life" of the new technologies, themselves. Library leaders of the future will have to be stimulated, rather than frustrated, by such contradictions and challenged by the prospect of making sense, on a case-by-case basis, despite them. The role of the library leader is to carve a workable path through a thicket of paradoxes, not to permit them to become obstacles or (even worse) to deny their existence.

Brown University President Vartan Gregorian makes this point (and identifies another paradox) when he writes, "The new information technologies are a driving force behind both the explosion of information and the fragmentation of knowledge . . . They let us easily organize ourselves into ever more specialized communities . . . the role of the (university) president is . . . to establish a process that will promote the integration of these new technologies, both with each other and with the mission and core values of the university. It is one of active moral and intellectual leadership."[8] This statement applies as logically to today's library director, regardless of the setting in which s/he functions. How can a library director lead in an age of paradox? By using paradox itself as a tool and as a teaching device. A project to digitize manuscript and other special collections materials and make them accessible via the Internet, as recently highlighted through the Vatican Library Exhibit at the Library of Congress, demonstrates not only the possibilities of the technology, but the value of having preserved and maintained the original sources. When librarians participate as partners with computing experts in the design of a campus wide information system (CWIS), as they have done at Brown University, Dartmouth College, the University of Southern California, the University of San Diego, and elsewhere, it not only highlights the value of a librarian's professional expertise, but demonstrates its applicability to a new means of showcasing information. If we believe that librarian assistance is *more* critical today rather than less, a library leader can make an effort to translate this assistance to a new knowledge environment, whether through electronic mail, the online catalog, or some other mechanism. An excellent example of innovative thinking in this regard is the "knowledge management" model developed by Richard Lucier, University Librarian and Vice Chancellor for Academic Information at the University of California-San Francisco, in concert with Nina Matheson. In this model, librarians take an active role with faculty and other researchers at the beginning of the information process rather than at its end, assisting in the development and structuring of databases even as research is ongoing.[9] Librarians thus become creators, as well as conservators, of knowledge. All these examples overcome today's paradoxes and ambiguities in favor of carrying forward "the idea of a library," making use of traditional strengths in a non-traditional way.

Another essential quality we should look for in the future information services leader is *vision, but vision in harness with practical political and communication skills.* Vision is critical, in that one who would lead must certainly have a sense of where s/he wants to go, but what may be more important is the ability to place one's vision in the context of community values as outlined above, the competence to articulate that vision to staff, administration, and users, and a practical sense of how to get things done within the organization. Vision is of little value if it cannot be translated into a specific action plan which results in the delivery of practical services to those who seek information. Richard Chait recognized this, again in terms of college presidents, when in an article entitled "Colleges Should Not be Blinded by Vision," he quoted IBM CEO Louis V. Gerstner, Jr.: "A vision is often what somebody turns to when it gets hard doing what's required–namely, good, solid blocking and tackling. Remember, the Wizard of Oz was a vision."[10]

In developing a vision, it is necessary to remain closely in touch with our users, lest we get what is technically *possible* confused with user needs and priorities. The best library leaders have always been those who had a realistic understanding of the many and varied ways in which their users experienced the library, and this is unlikely to change. Chemists, historians and political scientists, for example, do not see the library in the same way and are unlikely to be equally impressed, or well served, by an identical "information services" package in the future, however technically sophisticated. The information services vision which drives planning in a research library may be quite different, but no better, than the vision which motivates a community college, public, or secondary school library. In keeping with this understanding, the State University of New York University Center libraries, through a grant from the Council on Library Resources, recently completed a study of "the changing needs, attitudes, and expectations of faculty for library and information services."[11] More than 1,000 faculty members responded to the survey, which found, among other things, that while a significant number of faculty had access to personal computers and made use of online information sources, "only two-thirds of the faculty are connected to the campus network from their offices, and fewer than one-third are linked to the network from their homes." The study also found that humanities faculty had "significantly less campus access to computer and communications equipment than (did) their counterparts in the sciences, social sciences, and in professional schools," a pattern which is consistent with that identified in other studies.[12] Information services leaders in the SUNY system, if they wish to carry forward "the idea of a library" to the future, will need to plan within the context of these realities and (as they have recommended), address the issues of campus networking and faculty connectivity before a more ambitious future can be realized. We require vision in our information services leaders, indeed, but vision informed by a good sense of the needs and interests of our particular user community. This is not to say that we cannot, from time to time, encourage our users toward an information future they have not foreseen; in doing so, however, we would be wise to make sure that we have addressed our community's most critical perceived needs along the way.

Nor must vision be disconnected from a real willingness to plunge in and tackle the myriad complex, mundane and sometimes unpleasant details which must be addressed if the vision is to become reality. Perhaps one could characterize this necessary quality as *tenacity, or persistence, or even patience.* Many of us have had experiences with eloquent and charismatic individuals who could envision and articulate a future, but who lacked the patience, application, and political skills necessary to lead the organization to it. Some would-be leaders are excited by painting pictures of what it will be like when tomorrow comes, but find questions about "But what are we going to do today?" and "How can we afford to do that?" irritating. Yet these questions must be addressed if the library is to make a successful transition from what it is today to what it has the promise of becoming. Users are unlikely to support the upheavals necessary to create the library of the future if today's transitional phase is so poorly handled that services are perceived as declining, rather than improving, and our peer administrators will hardly volunteer to have resources transferred to information-related projects, at the expense of their own priorities, without some sense that it is in their own interest. In his book *On Leadership,* John Gardner says, "A familiar failure of visionaries and of people who live in the realm of ideas and issues is that they are not inclined to soil their hands with the nuts and bolts of organizational functioning. Often there is a snobbish element involved. Some are inclined to believe that the people who work in the subbasements of power and understand the organizational machinery are lesser people. Good leaders do not ignore the machinery. Every leader needs some grasp of how to work the system."[13] Gardner's words are particularly pertinent to the information services leader of the future because the 21st Century library will not arrive without a substantial investment of money, energy, political capital, and time. The successful information services leader, today and tomorrow, will be the one who can "work the system" so as to obtain user, staff, and administrative support for this investment, who can continue an acceptable level of service for today while leading users, and staff, toward the future, and who can persist in the face of roadblocks, frustrations, and setbacks. The exigencies of today cannot be ignored while we construct the superior, future information system (assuming that today we know what that will be), and getting where we want to go is an incremental, rather than a transformational, process.

Coming to terms with this reality–the incremental nature of information progress–may be more critical than it appears. Often the prospects of the *future* are more appealing, to funding agencies, university administrators, and librarians, than are the mundane problems of the present. When it comes to finding resources, for example, it may be easier to "sell" a university administration and alumni donors on the idea of investing in equipment and software for the 21st Century information system than it is to obtain a much more modest sum to support enhanced service and document delivery in the interlibrary loan office today. Yet, faculty and students who are frustrated in their attempts to get information from outside sources in a timely fashion will be slow to buy into the promise of a virtual library, and to support the administration in an effort to transfer funds from traditional acquisitions to electronic access. The skilled information services leader must establish a clear connection, for staff and community alike, between where we are today and where we want to go. To again cite Handlin, "the librarian has a kind of heritage . . . he does not walk among blank shelves"–in services as in collections.

Flexibility and a talent for teamwork and building alliances are additional key qualities for the information services leaders of tomorrow. Flexibility will be important in designing new organizational structures, in looking at new economic models, in considering what defines a librarian, and, perhaps most importantly, in working with information itself. Librarianship has been a profession founded in great part on rules and on the ability to organize and categorize, and these abilities will remain important in the future, but perhaps in different ways. In the past, information came to that library building/ organization of which we spoke earlier, where it was captured, categorized and presented for use by those who made their way through our doors. In a sense, library users were our hostages, forced to play the game our way, on our premises, if they expected to retrieve what they needed from the collections. While librarians always attempted to make decisions with the good of "the user" foremost, how successful we really were in making our collections–especially those of large libraries–easily usable is open to debate. As a profession, we have placed great emphasis on consistency, attention to detail, and order. We have been less receptive to experimentation, risk, and, if you will, access at the expense of detailed cataloging and other record keeping. The "up" side of the situation was the ability to exert some control over a large volume of information; the "down" side included backlogs of information which our own complex systems made it impossible to process quickly, classification systems which made sense for some disciplines but not for others, and access schemes which put off as many users as they assisted. Today, we face a world where users are presented with far more options for obtaining information, where they may to some extent design their own approaches to the world of knowledge, and where they need not, in many cases, set foot in the library. Furthermore, information no longer presents itself in packages which fit nicely within our existing cataloging schemes (ask the cataloger who has to prepare a location record for the last online serial your library purchased).

The task of the information services leader, in this world, is to find a way to link traditional and electronic resources, to assist the user, and to retain some degree of order, *without* clinging to a need for control in cases where control no longer makes sense. Here again, Campus Wide Information Systems (CWIS's) provide a useful example. At the user interface, a local CWIS may benefit from a structure developed by librarians, who are familiar with a variety of ways to organize information; yet, once launched into the CWIS, the user may wander into a number of "alien" data bases which are unlikely to be under local control. Is this a problem, or does it, in effect, provide the user with an information buffet from which s/he may select according to taste? Both, actually, and the task of an information leader, at least in the library, is to encourage staff to view the CWIS, and similar electronic marvels, more as a frontier to be explored and (perhaps) civilized than as a wilderness to be feared and avoided. The Internet can benefit from the notions of order as traditionally represented by librarians; librarians can benefit by the fresh approaches to presenting information to be discovered via the Internet.

Barbara von Wahlde and Nancy Schiller, in a paper entitled "Creating the Virtual Library: Strategic Issues," make the point that the next significant role for librarians may be as facilitators, organizing information at an early stage in the publication process so that users can find it themselves. They predict that much of the work currently performed by librarians will be taken over by support staff, while librarians "engage in developing the new systems and services of the virtual library, such as gateways, user interfaces, search and retrieval systems, tools for navigating the networks, and document delivery systems."[14] An overview of library newsletters, as they cross one's desk, easily substantiates this hypothesis, as even today a substantial amount of our staffs' time appears to be devoted to projects of this nature. The University of California-San Diego Libraries Newsletters (Fall 1993) describes not only InfoPath, the University CWIS, but a prospective project to digitize non-print media, "linking images with text, digitizing video, and supporting the engineering faculty's explorations of dynamic methods of accessing image and video through sophisticated computer-based techniques."[15] At SUNY Albany, the Fall 1993 *Library Update* contains articles not only about a new online information system in development, but about SUNY Express, a rapid document delivery system recently established.[16] It is clear that, in working to plan for these new information services, libraries are being flexible both about format, the nature of the modern "collection," and the role of librarians.

These projects serve to illustrate the importance of another leadership quality for future information services, and that is *a talent for teamwork and building alliances*. It is not necessary to repeat here the many points which have been made in the library literature about how the new information technologies are expected to alter library organizations. Suffice it to say that there is every indication that traditional, functional lines may be eradicated, that organizations will become less hierarchical, and that, to quote Von Wahlde and Schiller, "leadership and expertise will reside at all levels," while "Working relationships will be based on a team approach."[17] This observation becomes even more acute if one pauses a moment to consider the "library without walls," the library as an idea, not as a building or an organization. *That* library will depend upon a series of relationships and alliances, both within our parent organizations and outside them; the library without walls will exist, in a manner of speaking, "within the web." It will require leaders, then, who have all the talents of team players, including the ability to persuade, to negotiate, to overcome concerns about "turf," and to focus on the central goal, not on what is best for oneself or one's unit. In a speech given at the University of North Carolina at Chapel Hill, Patricia Battin, President of the Commission on Preservation and Access, commented that twenty years ago, universities used to view the position of library director as a "job with major responsibilities for the internal operations of an autonomous unit within the institution," whereas today "the traditional skills have been overtaken by the need for innovative leadership, effective communication skills, and (the ability to work) *with a broad range of institutional and external organizations.*"[18] She goes on to make the point that, today, the vast majority of the problems library directors face–from rising serial prices to the emergence of new technologies to basic changes in the nature of scholarly communication–cannot be resolved within the library, and that "we must view the delivery of information services from a system-wide perspective as a seamless web no longer separable into autonomous divisions . . . the organizational structure must . . . reflect the reality of the environment, which is one of inescapable inter-relationships among university officers, technology specialists, faculty, students and librarians."[19] If one were to extend Ms. Battin's analogy beyond the boundaries of the university campus, one would add publishers, vendors, software providers, and other information stakeholders to the list. Whatever the setting, it is clear that the autonomous library leader of the past, the individual who could make many decisions without consultation beyond the library and who had a clear idea of where the library's responsibilities began and ended, is a model not likely to be successful today, much less in the future.

There are, of course, many qualities that combine to make a successful leader, and the individual importance of these qualities varies according to the situation in which a given individual is placed. In concluding this article, however, we need to highlight one last, essential quality for future information services leaders, and that is something which could be categorized as *courage, or zest, or as "an attitude that embraces change and welcomes challenges."*[20] Human nature does not necessarily regard change as benign, and yet those of us who have chosen information services as a profession have signed on to a world where change is, and will be, a constant. Whatever our natural inclinations or our love for tradition–or our preference for finishing one project before we plunge on to the next one–we need to recognize that life from here on out will be a series of shocks and adjustments, some minor and some substantial, as we struggle to bring the "idea of the library" into the 21st Century. It will not be easy, it will not be without risk, and, as in any adventure, there will be elements beyond our capacity to control. What we need on this journey, at all levels, is leaders who want to set the course and help steer the ship, not head for the lifeboats. We need to recruit, and develop, staff who enter the profession not for security or structure but for intellectual excitement and the opportunity to shape a new world, and we need to begin to seek out, and reward, creativity and energy in the same way that we have traditionally valued experience, professional knowledge, and reliability. Gerald R. Lowell, University Librarian and Associate Vice Chancellor for Academic Information Technology at UC San Diego, said it well:

> You know, I used to fear flying, perhaps because I had no direct control over my destiny while up in the air. With patience, hard work, and a great deal of flexibility on my part, I've learned to overcome this discomfort and am now able to focus on the adventure associated with travel. I've found that leading the library within this changing world of digitization and an emergent information infrastructure requires similar patience, flexibility, and hard work. We don't have all of the answers; we don't have the perfect delivery mechanisms in place; we don't know all that awaits us in coming years. But we are being rewarded with great adventures. The ways in which we access and use information are changing dramatically, thanks to a host of technological wonders. All of us will be involved in these changes, so "keep your seatbelts fastened."[21]

NOTES

1. James Gleick, "The Telephone Transformed–Into Almost Everything," *The New York Times Magazine,* May 16, 1993: 27-28.

2. Gleick 27-28.

3. Oscar Handlin, "The Idea of a Library," *Celebrating the Acquisition of the Two Millionth Volume of the State University of New York at Buffalo Libraries,* eds. Robert J. Bertholf and Stephen M. Roberts (Buffalo, NY: 1983), N. pag.

4. Handlin 6-7.

5. Robin Alston, "The Battle of the Books," *Humanist Discussion Group* (online conference) 7, no. 176 (September 10, 1993), N. pag.

6. Harlan Cleveland, *The Knowledge Executive: Leadership in an Information Society* (New York, Truman Talley Books/E. P. Dutton, 1985) 5.

7. Cleveland xvi.

8. Vartan Gregorian, Brian L. Hawkins, and Merrily E. Taylor, "Integrating Information Technologies: A Research University Perspective," *Cause/Effect* 15:4 (Winter 1992): 7.

9. Barbara von Wahlde and Nancy Schiller, "Creating the Virtual Library: Strategic Issues," *The Virtual Library: Visions and Realities*, ed. Laverna M. Saunders (Westport, CT., Meckler, 1993), 10.

10. Richard Chait, "Colleges Should Not Be Blinded by Vision," *Chronicle of Higher Education,* September 22, 1993: B1-2.

11. Thomas J. Galvin, "Electronic Information Access Technologies: A Faculty Needs Assessment," University at Albany/SUNY *Library Update* (Fall 1993): 3.

12. Galvin 3.

13. Gardner 65.

14. von Wahlde and Schiller 24-25.

15. Gerald R. Lowell, "Librarian's Letter," *UCSD Libraries Newsletter* 11:1 (Fall 1993): 4.

16. David A. Tyckoson, "SUNY Express Takes Off," University at Albany/SUNY *Library Update* (Fall 1993): 4.

17. von Wahlde and Schiller 23.

18. Patricia Battin, "Changing Boundaries," The Research Library Director: Twenty Years of Change, a symposium honoring Dr. James F. Govan, Wilson Library, University of North Carolina at Chapel Hill, October 19, 1992.

19. Battin.

20. von Wahlde and Schiller 21.

21. Lowell 4.

REFERENCES

Alston, Robin. "The Battle of the Books." *Humanist Discussion Group* 7, no. 176, September 10, 1993. Online conference.

Battin, Patricia. "Changing Boundaries." The Research Library Director: Twenty Years of Change: A symposium honoring Dr. James F. Govan. Wilson Library, University of North Carolina at Chapel Hill, October 19, 1992.

Chait, Richard. "Colleges Should Not Be Blinded by Vision." *Chronicle of Higher Education,* September 22, 1993: B1-2.

Cleveland, Harlan. *The Knowledge Executive: Leadership in an Information Society.* New York: Truman Talley Books/E. P. Dutton, 1985.

Galvin, Thomas J. "Electronic Information Access Technologies: A Faculty Needs Assessment." University at Albany/SUNY *Library Update* (Fall 1993), 3.

Gardner, John. *On Leadership.* New York, Free Press, 1990.

Gleick, James. "The Telephone Transformed—Into Almost Everything." *The New York Times Magazine* May 16, 1993: 26-62.

Gregorian, Vartan, Brian L. Hawkins, and Merrily E. Taylor. "Integrating Information Technologies: A Research University Perspective." *Cause/Effect* 15 (Winter 1992): 5-12.

Handlin, Oscar. "The Idea of a Library." *Celebrating the Acquisition of the Two Millionth Volume of the State University of New York at Buffalo Libraries.* Eds. Robert J. Bertholf and Stephen M. Roberts. Buffalo, NY, 1983. N. pag.

Lowell, Gerald R. "Librarian's Letter." *UCSD Libraries Newsletter* (Fall 1993), 1-4.

Tyckoson, David A. "SUNY Express Takes Off." University at Albany/SUNY *Library Update* (Fall 1993), 4.

von Wahlde, Barbara and Nancy Schiller. "Creating the Virtual Library: Strategic Issues." *The Virtual Library: Visions and Realities.* Ed. Laverna M. Saunders. Westport, CT., Meckler, 1993. 15-46.

Systems Thinking
in Information Service Delivery

Carolyn M. Gray

INTRODUCTION

Libraries face many challenges today in integrating technology and information services. I wish to reflect on some of these challenges while considering the organization and role of the library systems staff in relation to public service staff in information systems and service delivery. The paper will draw upon my experience at the Brandeis Libraries and refer to relevant management literature in an attempt to provide some insight into how library organizations might bring about significant changes in the structure and effectiveness of information services.

This paper outlines the features of an information services unit that is functionally integrated with systems staff and suggests measures that libraries can take to organize for success in today's library environment. Four guiding principles are identified and discussed which are useful in providing leadership and direction in information services. The principles are summarized below:

- Assess the organizational environment;
- Establish normative criteria;

Carolyn M. Gray is Associate Director for Public Services at Brandeis University Libraries, Waltham, MA.

[Haworth co-indexing entry note]: "Systems Thinking in Information Service Delivery." Gray, Carolyn M. Co-published simultaneously in *Journal of Library Administration* (The Haworth Press, Inc.) Vol. 20, Nos. 3/4, 1995, pp. 25-43; and: *The Future of Information Services* (ed: Virginia Steel, and C. Brigid Welch) The Haworth Press, Inc., 1995, pp. 25-43. Multiple copies of this article/chapter may be purchased from The Haworth Document Delivery Center [1-800-3-HAWORTH; 9:00 a.m. - 5:00 p.m. (EST)].

- Promote learning organization principles; and
- Establish decision-making structure.

WHY WE MUST CHANGE–TODAY'S CHALLENGES

Libraries have been stable organizations and have demonstrated adaptive learning capacity by changing and improving incrementally in response to changes in publishing, in technology, in the work force, and in service demands. However, this is not a stable time for libraries, and adaptive learning is no longer sufficient to meet today's multiple and complex challenges. Libraries, generally, have been conservative about radically altering traditional organizational structures. In a 1984 essay in *Reference Services and Technical Services: Interactions in Library Practice,* Michael Gorman suggests breaking down the barriers between technical services and reader services by taking an ecumenical approach to library organization. He says, "we should work . . . to abolish the division between technical and public services and to create structures in which groups of librarians are defined not by which aspect of professional librarianship they practice (cataloguing, reference work, etc.) but by the area of service in which they exercise their skills across the whole range of professional librarianship"(Gorman, 1984). Ten years later, only modest progress has been made in breaking down the internal organizational barriers in libraries. In the intervening years, there have been many forces exerting pressures on libraries and suggesting the need for change.

Four particularly noteworthy trends give a flavor of the diversity and complexity of issues facing libraries. Trends that have been most challenging for us at Brandeis include: technological innovations, economic shifts, publishing growth and complexity, and calls for public accountability. Since these trends have been discussed in the popular and scholarly press in detail, I wish to limit my coverage to the impact of these trends in libraries, particularly in information services.

Technological innovations in recent years include something for everyone in the library–online searching in remote databases created and maintained by BRS or DIALOG, the introduction of mainframe computers for handling transaction data, the revolution of cataloging through OCLC, microcomputers on the desk top, CD-ROM LANs in reference, the Internet, integrated library computer systems, and electronic imaging systems, to name a few. Technology impacts service delivery, financial control, and staff. The introduction in libraries of many of these systems and services has markedly improved productivity, especially in cataloging, circulation, and interlibrary loan. Within the last few years the impact has been felt strongly in information services–changing the nature of the librarian/client interactions. Technology has also changed the staffing needs in information services. Technically skilled staff are needed whether that is through recruitment, training, transfers, or collaboration with systems staff.

Economic trends include the costs of library resources, the general recession, and taxpayer revolt. Costs for scholarly books and journals have skyrocketed in recent years. Over the years, libraries have been steadily reducing book purchases in an effort to maintain critically important journal subscriptions, while at the same time we have experienced an increasing demand for electronic resources. The economics of higher education are forcing cutbacks of staff at a time when demands on library services are increasing dramatically and more trained staff are needed for user education and for better management of dwindling acquisition dollars. Economics, to some extent, is driving libraries to look for partners in resource sharing, which requires shifts in thinking and approaches among information services and collection development staffs alike.

Publishing growth continues at an unprecedented rate. The diversity in format and source of information is also growing. The increasing volume and complexity of information sources presents continual challenges to staff and users alike. These publishing trends make the selection process for resources in the reference collection increasingly complex. It requires systems consultation to decide on the equipment necessary to mount electronic resources, consultation with collections staff in regard to cost and permanence of resource being selected, and information services consultation in regard to how the resource is going to be utilized by both librarians and clients in service delivery. These decisions must be collaborative and require good working relations among the various areas of responsibility.

Public accountability has become a part of our collective consciousness–one only has to pay attention to the news. One day it is the scandal of 100%+ overhead rates being charged by some private universities against government grants. The next day it is about public officials taking junkets to exotic places at taxpayers' expense. We hold corporations accountable for their environmental disasters and teachers responsible for the education of our children. Whether there is actually more accountability can be debated, but the fact is, accountability has become a part of our public and private discourse. At a private university such as Brandeis, with among the highest tuition costs in the nation, we are well aware of our accountability to the administration, students, faculty, and funding sources. We can no longer assume it is a given that we will get increases in funding by maintaining standard operating procedures. We are listening to what users say about our services through focus groups and other research and evaluation efforts. We must make service decisions based on facts not just intuition.

In sum, these trends mean that we have less money to spend on a greater array of library resources and less money to install more and better technology, plus we must do so with greater accountability to our users and funding sources. Some of us view these challenges as opportunities for innovation. As we began to grapple with these challenges, we developed a "Service Strategies White Paper" in which we identified four key strategies for providing library services. We determined that we would focus on access to information, technological innovation, library instruction, and staff development. We see these as the key service strategies necessary for innovation and vitality in light of the tremendous challenges posed by the trends outlined. The following section describes the information services model we have adopted at Brandeis to carry out the service strategies.

INFORMATION SERVICES–A TEAM-BASED APPROACH

Libraries add value to information by being people centered–not technology centered. Technology offers a powerful set of tools and ever increasing seductive options, but we must be guided by vision if we are to use the tools effectively. My vision is a library that is:

service-oriented; integrated into the life of the community it serves; staffed by a responsive, knowledgeable group of creative individuals who have technical skills, subject expertise, and human relations skills; stocked with comprehensive collections; equipped with the latest technologies to offer information from a broad array of resources; financed adequately; and supported by the community.

The people, service, and technology portions of this vision can only be achieved if we question assumptions and change standard operating procedures in libraries. The integration of systems staff into information services is one step. The nature of information services today requires technological support in management, user education, and reference services. Systems staff have technical knowledge and skills needed in user services, and information services staff have knowledge of the needs of users, valuable in creating better information systems. To integrate systems staff into a traditional information services unit creates a staff with varied sets of skills and knowledge and different orientations. The challenge is to fashion creative and effective information services units in our libraries with this diverse mix of experience, skills and knowledge.

The nature of work in the traditional reference department has changed radically in recent years as a direct result of technological innovations. The information and guidance roles of librarians increasingly requires the use of technology. User education, training, and use of libraries all require the use of technology. In a typical academic library it is not uncommon for reference staff to use ten to twelve different computer systems, each with different search software, to help users who are overwhelmed by the variety and complexity of information technologies available. Users need and demand more instruction from librarians on new technologies, on information services available, on library research, and on evaluating information sources. The old models of assisting users primarily through one-to-one encounters at the reference desk are no longer adequate or effective. This complexity stimulated us to develop and refine a research consultation model of providing service. (See Herman, 1993 and Figure 3.) As a complement to research consultation a library intensive-teaching program has also been developed and is a regular part of a librarian's duties. (See Figure 1 for an outline of the library intensive program.)

FIGURE 1. Library Intensive Instruction

Library intensive instruction consists of:

1. Preliminary conferences with instructors on the design of assignments, new information technologies, and relevant resources;

2. Formal group instruction of students;

3. Individual consultation with students, printed guides, and assistance in using off-campus resources; and

4. Feedback to faculty about students' experiences in completing assignments.

From:
Brandeis University Libraries
Library Instruction Program

Information services librarians require not only technical searching skills, but they must have a general comfort level with computers. They must be able to handle paper jams in a half dozen different types of printers, download records and data from dozens of different electronic sources, re-boot computers, load and unload compact disks, possess a basic knowledge of DOS and many other technical tasks necessary to ensure the electronic tools are available to the public and they must be able to help users effectively. It is not always possible to have a systems person on hand to handle the myriad technical tasks that crop up on a busy afternoon in the reference department. These technical skills must be combined with subject expertise, if librarians are to provide high quality services to the users. A team-based approach to organization is one good way of building the skill and knowledge base of all members while addressing the day-to-day service issues.

Cross-functional teams made up of information services, technical services, and systems staff are useful in planning and implementing systems for public access. The team establishes requirements for the system. The systems staff portion of the team translates the requirements into workable systems in constant consultation with the entire team. The team as a whole implements systems for patron use. Information services members of the team develop documentation and training for the public. Technical services members organize and change processing procedures as appropriate. Systems staff understand the information technology field, traditional librarian skills relate to organization and dissemination of information, and information services staff should have an understanding of client needs. To be truly effective, the team must have both responsibility and authority to act–often referred to as team-based management.

Cross functional learning also occurs in these teams. Systems staff teach information service delivery personnel some of the analytical skills necessary to engage in systems thinking. Information services staff teach systems staff client-focused approaches to design. Systems staff tend to have good conceptual thinking skills, that is, in the mental formulation of ideas. Information services staff tend to be better at perceptual thinking–applying insight or intuition to problem solving. However, if the team is truly learning together, there will be a good balance between conception and intuition.

For ongoing operations, we have found it beneficial to make sure that at least one information services librarian is also a member of the systems staff. This began at Brandeis a few years ago as a matrix reporting structure and is evolving into a team-based management approach. Some staff have actually moved from one department to another, and some still report in multiple departments. The skills that are exchanged by this fluid movement of staff is beneficial to all concerned. Librarians who have spent many of their professional years in a catalog department approach bibliographic questions differently from librarians who go into reference departments right out of library school. Experience in cataloging creates a deeper understanding of the structure of knowledge and how it is described within the various bibliographic tools. Experience in systems creates a deeper understanding of the underlying structure of computer programs and of the various systems we use on a regular basis. These diverse viewpoints bring depth to the services we are able to provide our clients.

If this management structure seems a bit fluid and imprecise, it is because that is the case. Not everyone is comfortable with the level of ambiguity required to operate in a transitional organizational structure, especially when some of the organization is still very traditionally organized. It requires staff who can live with a good deal of cognitive dissonance.

The final half of this paper outlines four principles that we have found helpful in providing leadership and direction while addressing organizational change. As of this writing, we expect that it will take us another five years to achieve our goals. We do not know what the organizational structure will actually look like when we finish, but we are committed to achieving excellence. The following is prepared as a helpful guide for others grappling with the same issues.

PRINCIPLES FOR PROVIDING LEADERSHIP AND DIRECTION

In the planning stages and during the transitional period, we have found the following principles to be especially helpful in providing leadership and direction:

1. *Assess the organizational environment.* To bring about positive organizational change requires an understanding of the organizational environment and climate. We have looked at the management literature for guidance in seeking options suitable for the Brandeis Libraries.
2. *Establish normative criteria.* Normative criteria forms the basis for programmatic development.
3. *Promote learning organization principles.* Regardless of the organizational structure, the principles of the learning organization are powerful tools for the development of staff, both individually and as a group.
4. *Establish an appropriate decision-making structure.* To be effective, organizations must have an appropriate decision-making structure to fit the form of the organization.

Assess Organizational Environment and Climate

A quick review of the evolution of management thought in this century will be helpful in understanding the theoretical foundations of the learning organization and why a library might aspire to become one. Changes in management theory since the early part of this century have had an impact on library organizations. Cargill and Webb (1988) note that as organizations' libraries have become more complex and library directors have become more involved in external relations, directors have had to delegate some of their decision-making authority. New management structures have to be created to accommodate these shifts.

As a part of our investigation into organizational structures, we examined the literature and sought the advice of experts. In an attempt to provide some insight into the evolution of management thought, we prepared a synthesis as a basis for discussion. That synthesis is represented in Figure 2 which outlines some of the major management theories that have been applied in organizational practice. The left-hand column lists the school of thought in rough chronological order of development. The right-hand column attempts to capture the method for measuring effectiveness utilized by each school of thought followed by the principal proponents of the theory.

Beginning with scientific management, we can see early efforts to bring efficiency and control into industries. Time studies were conducted to determine the most efficient way of accomplishing specific tasks. In the 1920s, an understanding began to emerge that there was a link between the welfare of the individual worker and job performance. The famous Hawthorne studies were conducted to determine the effect of proper lighting on performance. Increased or optimal lighting appeared to stimulate better job performance, then when the lighting was decreased to sub-optimal level, performance continued to improve–to the surprise of the researchers. A part of what was learned from the studies was that people do better work when someone pays attention to them–thus, it was discovered that the act of being studied introduces bias, known as the "Hawthorne Effect." After the Hawthorne studies brought some of the psycho-social issues into focus, there was a period of transition before and during the World War II period. During this period there was an attempt to develop socio-technical systems that incorporated the best of scientific management and human relations theories along with more refined management tools. Control charts were much in

FIGURE 2. Changes in Management Theory	
School of Thought	*Effectiveness Focus*
Scientific Management	Control and efficiency (Taylor, 1916)
Human Relations or Human Behavior	Interface between individual and organization (Hawthorne, 1920)
Socio-technical Control Charts Statistical Theory	Optimization of both technical and social systems (various, 1924-45)
Organizational Development	Interpersonal and inter-group linkages with openness of communication and teamwork (Bennis, Benne, & Chin, 1960s)
Microeconomics	Profit and return on investment (Friedman, 1970s)
Goal Attainment	Productivity, results, or ultimate goals
Systems Theory Open Systems Theory	Interdependencies of multiple factors and functions (Simon, 1946; Kahn, 1966)
Change Model	Ability of organization to bring about desired changes (Lewin, 1951)
Japanese Quality Movement Quality Circles	Product quality through teamwork at the operational level (Deming, Juran, 1954)
Transformational Leadership	Leaders who can constructively bring about change (Ticky, 1986)
Empowerment	Participation in the workplace. Workers are given power and authority over the way their work is organized (Warren Bennis, outgrowth of earlier OD school)
Total Quality Management Customer Service	Satisfaction of multiple constituencies in a continuous process of strategic renewal (Peters, 1982; various, 1980s)
The Learning Organization	Ability of organization to modify behavior as a result of new knowledge (Senge, 1990)

vogue throughout the "war effort," as was the application of the emerging field of statistical theory.

Systems theory began to emerge in the late 1940s and was adopted by the new electronic data processing field. As the theory evolved over the next twenty years, some confused the application of systems theory in the management field with the application of computer systems in organizations. It should be recognized, however, that systems theory has a much broader meaning, and it is fortunate that in many instances, the training that library systems staff have received incorporates a broader analytical approach. During the social reform and activist period of the 1960s, there was the growth of the organizational development field. T-groups, interpersonal and inter-group linkages developed with an emphasis on openness, communication, and teamwork. At the same time there was emerging a conservative, market-focused approach to organizations with the emphasis on microeconomic theory with its goals of profit and return on investments. And in Japan, the quality movement was in full swing. The Japanese quality movement emphasized product quality through teamwork.

In America, the organizational change model grew out of the organizational development field. Over a twenty-year period, three strategies for organizational change emerged in organizations. The empirical-rational strategy is based on the assumption that most people are rational and will follow their best interests. The normative-reeducative strategy is based on the assumption that people seek immediate satisfaction and are guided by the normative structure. This strategy emphasizes experience based learning as an ingredient if enduring change is to be brought about. The power-coercive strategy uses organizational power to gain compliance for change. In the early 1980s, there was perceived to be a "crisis in leadership," and a number of writers began to talk about the need for strong transformational leaders. These leaders, by providing vision and direction were expected to constructively transform organizations, and they most often used a form of the normative-reeducative strategy for bringing about organizational change. In addition to strong leaders, there was a realization that workers needed a say in the workplace; this has been variously called empowerment and worker participation. The result of this movement has been a democratization of organizations with workers gaining power and authority over the way their work is organized. This democratization has become closely aligned with the Japanese quality movement and has manifested itself in American organizations as total quality management with its focus on customer service and satisfaction. The most recent entry into this evolutionary process is the move to develop learning organizations which build upon and integrate issues of leadership, worker empowerment, total quality management tools, and systems theory.

One can see that there has been a definite trend away from mechanistic approaches to management to a recognition that human resources are key to organizational success. Coupled with the trend of valuing people as employees has been a move to more customer-focused approaches in service delivery. Both technological innovations and increased customer focus have led some writers to suggest that the majority of librarians in the future will be working in direct client support, educating users, serving as research consultants, and providing information (Adams, 1986). The question for library administrators is how we might learn from these trends in our efforts to assess our own organizational environments and create new management structures. The learnings from this analysis support the team-based approach and integration of staff in information service delivery.

Establish Normative Criteria

One of the first steps in any form of organizational development is to clarify the mission of the organization. It is the mission that should drive programmatic development. It is important to create a shared vision and to develop service objectives, strategies, and performance measures in relation to the organizational mission. The mission and vision-based strategies serve as normative criteria for the examination of our organizations and services to create vital libraries to serve our communities in the years to come. In 1988, we went through an intensive strategic planning process and developed a strategic plan that has helped guide us through our recent efforts at organizational improvement. It was in that earlier document that much of the normative criteria was codified. The "Service Strategies White Paper" alluded to earlier was an attempt to revise some of our thinking in response to changes in the environment. A part of the normative criteria that has been codified for us is the value placed on people—our key to success in information service delivery.

Promote Learning Organization Principles

The changes taking place in libraries mirror the changes occurring in all knowledge- or technology-intensive businesses. Many organizational and management theorists suggest that organizations which must quickly adapt to rapidly changing environments must become learning organizations if they are to adapt and thrive into the 21st century. It is here suggested that libraries would do well to adopt the tools of the learning organization to grow and remain vital into the future. The tools described in the learning organization are helpful in developing the potential of the human resources in an organization.

Although a variety of definitions have been given for the learning organization, the most useful seems to be the following offered by David A. Garvin:

> A learning organization is an organization skilled at creating, acquiring, and transferring knowledge, and at modifying its behavior to reflect new knowledge and insights. (Garvin, 1993:80)

Senge (1993), the most well-known proponent, outlines five disciplines that are the core of the learning organization. They include personal mastery, shared vision, team learning, mental models, and systems thinking. I wish to briefly define and relate these five disciplines to the organization and delivery of information services.

Personal mastery is broadly defined as a process of continually learning and striving toward a vision of what is important and a clear understanding of your current state. Within the context of information service delivery, the quest for professional excellence entails the setting of personal goals and an understanding of personal strengths and weaknesses. There is a widening range of skills that must be mastered and knowledge required to deliver information services today. Writing in 1983, Kathleen Gunning outlined the computer search skills required for online searching and the user education skills needed for library instruction. She noted that computer searching requires analytical and vocabulary abilities combined with an understanding of command languages and the syndetic structure of databases, while user education requires teaching, presentation, and writing skills. In the early 1980s, libraries were struggling with how to incorporate these two separate services into reference departments. Many libraries created separate search units and separate user education units. This is simply no longer possible. Every information services librarian must incorporate computer searching and user education skills in his/her arsenal of reference skills to achieve professional excellence. Personal mastery in information services at its advanced state integrates analytical and perceptual-thinking skills.

Shared vision ensures that people are connected by common aspirations. An example of a shared vision developed by the information services librarians at Brandeis is illustrated in Figure 3. These "Characteristics of a Research Consultation Model" (Herman, 1993) are the outgrowth of a half-day retreat aimed at articulating an updated description and vision of our research consultation model of providing reference services. This process was a part of a much larger effort to evaluate the research consultation model.

Team learning is basically the mastery of dialogue and discussion as a group or team. The three primary dimensions of team learning are the ability to think insightfully about complex issues, the ability to take innovative and coordinated action, and the ability of the learning team to foster other learning teams. No one person can master everything, but as a group, staff can learn together through collaboration and team learning. See Figure 4 for an illustration of team learning in practice.

Mental models involve examining assumptions and developing reflection and inquiry skills. Our assumptions limit the range of actions that we are willing to consider when attempting to make decisions and solve problems. If we can hold our assumptions in suspension, we may be able to examine them objectively, let others examine them, and not be bound by them. The process of developing reflection and inquiry skills is necessary to get beyond advocating one's point of view. When we can inquire into the views of others and balance that inquiry with appropriate advocacy for a particular point of view, we have a better chance of advancing the best argument and making better decisions. The Research Consultation Model requires librarians to suspend many of their assumptions about the role of a reference librarian. It is an ongoing process of

FIGURE 3. **Characteristics of a Research Consultation Model***

The principal emphasis of the Research Consultation Model of reference service is on teaching the basic research skills and the specific tools that comprise information literacy. The model favors those things that promote in-depth service–giving each patron's needs sufficient time and attention–over quickness of service and sheer availability.

Presentation of service: The reference area is physically designed to convey the idea that there are two distinct services being offered. The Information Desk is an outreach point where the general availability of help is made clear by having a service desk thrust out into the busiest part of the library, in the manner of a traditional reference desk. The consultation office, by contrast, is designed to offer the patron a measure of privacy and leisure. Patrons are invited to sit rather than stand, and their conversation is directed to the librarian alone, without the self-consciousness or interference that arises when reference questions are asked at a desk where more than one person is working and where several other patrons may be waiting. For the librarian, this atmosphere is intended to help in giving the individual patron's needs full and careful attention.

Reference interview: The value of a thorough reference interview is implicit in the model . . . .

Time: A walk-in research consultation has an approximate limit of twenty minutes when other patrons are waiting . . . . (Request for Information forms have been designed for the graduate students to take questions from patrons or for librarians to use if more follow-up is required.) . . . Appointments with individual librarians are sometimes offered, especially in cases where the need to keep re-stating a complex problem to a variety of librarians would be likely to obstruct progress. . .

Instruction: With the exception of some well-defined factual questions, reference questions are treated as opportunities for instruction. . . .

Collaboration: In theory, each librarian in the Main Library is responsible for all areas of the humanities and the social sciences, including the government document and legal collections. In practice, consultation with a colleague is always an option, either when a colleague has greater knowledge of a particular subject or collection, or when the librarian on duty simply feels stumped and would like a second opinion. Librarians will also consult with outside experts. .

Classes of Users and Questions: Most of the time librarians are able to devote equal time and effort to all reference questions. . . .

*From "Reference Services Evaluation Report" prepared by Douglas Herman, Brandeis University Libraries, June, 1993.

FIGURE 4
Praxis
Team Learning in Action

The *Oxford English Dictionary* on CD-ROM arrives in Reference this week. John, the humanities expert, assumes the job of learning how to use this entirely new kind of electronic reference tool. With the aid of Diane, the systems expert, the software is loaded on "learning machine." John spends a number of hours learning the system, when he is not on duty in Research Consultation or teaching a class. He talks with colleagues about what he is finding as they wander in to see what is new. Some librarians take time to explore on their own and ask questions as John is developing his expertise. Others may discover features and explore possibilities for use. In about a week or two, when John feels comfortable with the tool, he develops a training session and schedules it when most of the information services librarians can attend. The group meets together in the library instruction room, which is set up for electronic demonstrations, and John presents his material. Then the group begins to discuss what is similar to and what is different from other tools already in use in the information services area. Suggestions are made for additions to the training module, and the method of introducing the tool to the public and interested faculty and researchers is decided. The group discusses how this tool will be used in Research Consultation on a regular basis. The librarians are asked to practice what they have learned and they agree on a date for introduction to the public. All librarians will then be expected to incorporate use of this tool in their teaching and research consultation activities. John will develop any in-house documentation required, monitor usage and identify problems as the tool is introduced to the public. He may decide that a "refresher" or advanced session is needed, or one of the other librarians may request more individual help or a group session.

---

examination, dialogue, and discussion as our service delivery evolves.

The fifth discipline is systems thinking. Senge says, "Systems thinking is a conceptual framework, a body of knowledge and tools that has been developed over the past fifty years, to make the full patterns clearer, and to help us see how to change them effectively"(Senge, 1993:7).

In the late 1970s, C. West Churchman's *The Systems Approach* forever changed the way I think about libraries and the work we do. This work helped to shape my view of the library as an integrated system. Systems thinking is not a new approach, but one that has been used in a wide variety of organizations for many decades. Systems theory has been broadly and effectively used in strategic planning approaches to organizational analysis and improvement.

To solve most human problems, say the systems theorists, we must examine them systemically. To apply that view to libraries, we may observe that libraries are a part of a larger system of libraries, of scholarly communication, of education, and of the civic life of communities. Within the library, we use systems thinking to view the connections among the various tasks among library departments.

For generations now we have broken down the complex tasks of libraries into component parts in order to understand and design work units and systems to handle those tasks. In so doing, we have lost what Senge refers to as our "intrinsic sense of connection to a larger whole"(Senge, 1993:3). The integration of information service staff with systems staff is an attempt to regain the connection of the systems we design and operate to the front-line service workers who must interpret those systems to the public. This structural change is a natural outgrowth of systems thinking and represents an instance of seizing an opportunity to make those connections as electronic resources have moved from the "back room" to the "front room" of the library.

It is through the understanding, application, and integration of these learnings that we will begin to break down barriers between service units. The ability to suspend assumptions can help create a true dialogue within our libraries and within the library community. Information services is a good place to begin creating an integrated organization because the skills and knowledge needs are so immediate. The sheer volume of new material that must be learned and the technology that must be mastered demand new approaches and generative learning. Generative learning "emphasizes continuous experimentation and feedback in an ongoing examination of the very way organizations go about defining and solving problems"(McGill, Slocum and Lei: 1992:7). This is contrasted with adaptive learning which is slower in pace and more evolutionary than today's rapid pace of change demands.

Establish Adequate Decision-Making Structure

The decision-making structure should function in concert with the form of the organizational structure. Decision making must be team-based, if the organization is committed to moving to a team-based management approach. Systems thinking dictates that when teams are involved in decision making that may impact other individuals or work units, the team is required to consult with others. When the impact of a decision will be felt in other units, the team leader is obligated to seek input and build a consensus around the problem definition. Once there is consensus on the problem, then a solution can be proposed. This is at the heart of systems thinking and the team-based approach to management. The teams understand that they are a part of a larger whole, and individual team members are often members of multiple teams in overlapping or separate functional units. The earlier example of a decision to purchase an electronic reference tool suggested the participation of information services staff, systems staff, and collections staff–these types of decisions could be made by a cross-functional team established for just such a function.

The roles of a library director in this model are leadership and policy direction, resource procurement and stewardship.

CONCLUSION

This paper attempts to accomplish three things: (1) to illustrate that changes in the structure of information services are accomplished in the context of a larger organizational structure; (2) to outline a set of principles to be followed in bringing about organizational change; and (3) to introduce the reader to the principles of the learning organization as appropriate tools for organizational improvement.

Some of the benefits from efforts at organizational improvement such as have been described, especially in information services, include the excitement and engagement of staff, a renewed sense of appreciation from clients, empowerment of staff, interest and excitement of potential funding sources, and a renewed sense that the work we do is of importance. Librarians can try to cope with the changes taking place around us, or we can view the changes as opportunities for innovation–the choice is ours to make.

REFERENCES

Adams, Roy J. *Information Technology and Libraries: A Future for Academic Libraries.* London: Croom Helm, 1986.

Cargill, Jennifer and Gisela M. Webb. *Managing Libraries in Transition.* Phoenix, AZ: Oryx, 1988.

David A. Garvin. "Building a Learning Organization." *Harvard Business Review.* (July-August, 1993):78-91.

Gorman, Michael. "The Ecumenical Library." In *Reference Services and Technical Services: Interactions in Library Practice,* edited by Gordon Stevenson and Sally Stevenson. New York: The Haworth Press, Inc., 1984. 55-64.

Gunning, Kathleen. "The Impact of User Education and Computer Searching Programs on Reference Service." In *Reference Service: A Perspective,* edited by Sul H. Lee. Ann Arbor, MI: Pierian Press, 1983. 78-88.

Herman, Douglas. "Reference Evaluation Report." An unpublished internal report for the Brandeis University Libraries, 1993. Mr. Herman, who is Coordinator of Reference Services at Brandeis, compiled these characteristics from the notes of a staff retreat. He led the effort to evaluate the Research Consultation Model and is preparing for publication a description of the evaluation process and the outcomes from the study. The characteristics are quoted from the in-house presentation of findings prepared by Mr. Herman.

Massey-Burzio, Virginia. "Reference Encounters of a Different Kind: A Symposium." *The Journal of Academic Librarianship.* 8:5 (1992):276-286. The article describes the initial design of the Research Consultation Model, when Ms. Massey-Burzio was Head of Reference at Brandeis.

McGill, Michael, E. John W. Slocum, Jr., and David Lei. "Management Practice in Learning Organizations." *Organizational Dynamics* (Summer, 1992):5-17.

Senge, Peter M. *The Fifth Discipline: The Art and Practice of the Learning Organization.* New York: Doubleday, 1990.

Paving the Way:
Building a Community Electronic
Information Infrastructure

Kenneth H. Dowlin
Katherine N. Wingerson

HISTORY

Over the last hundred years, the public library has collected and organized a vast collection of printed and graphic records for the use of the community. Historically, here at San Francisco Public Library, we have seen our primary role as the acquisition and preservation of the printed record–the function of organization and expeditious access for the user had been a secondary role. However, over the past five years a major focus of the library staff and management has shifted to the inventory and organization of these many resources to increase access. The library is moving from *collection* to *access* in response to the major paradigm shifts: *scarcity vs. overabundance;* librarian as *gatekeeper vs. facilitator;* the library as *fortress vs. pipeline.*

Kenneth H. Dowlin holds MAs in Library Science from the University of Denver, and in Public Administration from the University of Colorado. He is currently the City Librarian of San Francisco Public Library. He is a past president of LITA and is the author of *The Electronic Library: The Promise and the Process.* Katherine N. Wingerson is Special Assistant to the City Librarian, San Francisco Public Library. She holds an MLIS from the University of California at Berkeley and an AB from the University of North Carolina, Chapel Hill.

[Haworth co-indexing entry note]: "Paving the Way: Building a Community Electronic Information Infrastructure." Dowlin, Kenneth H., and Katherine N. Wingerson. Co-published simultaneously in *Journal of Library Administration* (The Haworth Press, Inc.) Vol. 20, Nos. 3/4, 1995, pp. 45-55; and: *The Future of Information Services* (ed: Virginia Steel, and C. Brigid Welch) The Haworth Press, Inc., 1995, pp. 45-55. Multiple copies of this article/chapter may be purchased from The Haworth Document Delivery Center [1-800-3-HAWORTH; 9:00 a.m. - 5:00 p.m. (EST)].

45

Around the turn of the century books were still scarce resources. Bookstores were limited, and books were very expensive to purchase. Private libraries were the domain of the rich. The libraries of the time were organized around the theory that books were scarce and thus must be hoarded and shared. The library as an organization was formed to address scarcity of resources, but now must deal with an over-abundance of information.

The major public libraries were once known as the university of the poor. Older urban public libraries, such as Boston Public Library, have been honored for providing knowledge and reading skills to the waves of immigrants who entered this country in the last century. The library at that time was organized on the concept that the librarian, who was generally better educated than the general public, was the gatekeeper for the knowledge in the collection. This librarian possessed the traditional skills needed for that role and for the collection of books: acquisition, cataloging, processing, readers' advisory, reference, collection development, and planning. The library professional will have to transform older skills and develop new skills to address the changes required in facilitating access to the multiplicity of available information resources.

The traditional library service model required that the person needing the material or information go to library facilities for service. This required the library to provide branches that are convenient to every neighborhood, providing all library services in every branch. Today, in most cities, the cost of operating this traditional library system has outstripped the library's budget. In order to survive, the library must make a fundamental change in the way access is provided to the user. The new model must focus on networked access, differentiated levels of service, and direct delivery. The library must be a partner in the building of a local infrastructure for information, a Community Electronic Information Infrastructure (CEII), cognate to President Clinton's National Information Infrastructure (NII).

CURRENT ISSUES AND CHALLENGES

There are several societal and community changes that have dramatically impacted the public library: the shifts in our population's diversity and educational level, the public's perception of the public library, and the proliferation of communications media. The library's ability to draw in the user or compete for his/her attention has not kept pace with lifestyle changes. The net result of all this is the fact that the public library's market share has shrunk dramatically. Ironically, this has happened at the same time information needs have grown enormously, owing to the increasingly complex and global society.

Few people can cope with the technology tools today or make an informed decision about product consumption without multiple validated sources of information. Nor can they make an informed judgment about those who govern, or who invest their money, or who advise them about their health needs. The library's ability to cope with all of these trends is diminished because of increased cost-consciousness and the shrinking public support for government expenditures, forcing libraries to be more and more cost-effective.

Most major urban centers now have tremendous diversity in the neighborhoods and in their cultural institutions, and this diversity requires that the library deals with all of the languages not only in the collection, but in the community. For many new immigrants, the public library is one of their first contacts with the community outside of family. In order to catalog, inventory, and provide access to the collection, it is a requirement that the library have a state-of-the-art computer system with a multi-lingual on-line public access catalog.

Patrons' needs and expectations are changing rapidly. As people become more computer literate and are exposed to the idea of an "information infrastructure" and the high-speed data superhighway in popular magazines, they begin to expect their local library to provide access to the information and services these networks provide. The new cultures and languages that make up our communities constantly require changes in our way of doing business.

Today, there is a renewed commitment to making the library's resources available to all members of the community, particularly those with special information needs. The library must address all these changes to stay relevant, and technology is giving us the means to retain our stature in the community. The information needs that the library meets have shifted dramatically since the inception of the phrase "a free public library." Rather than organizing for the edification of the scholars and recreational readers in a slow-paced world, the library must participate in a fast-paced, ever-changing society. John Gardner contends that the future health of our society depends upon our ability to create communities that value diversity yet provide overarching values for the community as a whole. The public library can play a positive role in that future by securing equal access to information for our diverse communities.

The Internet's impact on the libraries throughout the world is just beginning to emerge. Within the first few years there are already thousands of library catalogs and databases available to virtually anyone who has a microcomputer, a modem, and an access point into the network. There is a revolution underway that will eventually impact the operation of every organization in the world. We posit that even with the dramatic increase in global electronic networking, there will not be one gigantic library in the electronic center of the world, but that libraries will continue to be mostly local institutions with real-time sharing of resources and customers. The public library that can position itself to take advantage of the opportunities offered by such networking will make itself invaluable to the community. The public library that chooses to ignore these opportunities may find itself marginalized.

STRATEGIES

In order to face the challenges, address the issues, and seize the opportunities that the changes in society and advances in technology offer, the library administrator must incorporate new strategies into his/her planning process. The administrator will need to create a vision for the library, taking into account the changes and challenges in our communities. The administration must reach out to create new partnerships with public and private organizations using innovative financing and support arrangements. To gain the greatest support from the community, the library must reach out to the community to learn of its needs and desires and then bring those affinity groups into the process. Using these strategies, the library can be a partner in the creation of the Community Electronic Information Infrastructure (CEII).

The vision of the 60s–a branch on every block–is no longer viable. We cannot live with our success of putting a scaled-down version of the Main Library in every neighborhood. This model costs too much, and lifestyle changes in the past thirty years challenge the appropriateness of this model. In order to survive so that we can address the challenges, the library must create a new vision at the local, state, and national levels. We need to engage and involve our communities, and take advantage of the opportunities for connectivity that technology offers. Library administrators need to paint a picture of what the library could be and what it takes to get there. The process of visioning needs to be collaborative with the community, but it also requires leadership from someone who has the ability to scan the broader environment, to spot trends, and to enlist support. It is critical that this process take place soon, since there are major resource shifts in the offing such as the tax shift in California, the re-authorization of LSCA, and any NII legislation in the coming session of Congress.

The leadership of the library must expand outreach to people and organizations not traditionally in the library's constituency. We have to partner with organizations that know how to do what we do not. We should learn from the experience and expertise of other types of organizations. The public library can discover how to build the partnerships, how to build the networks, and how to implement the technologies.

Another strategy requires a major shift in the organization move away from a paternal to a collaborative paradigm. The most effective strategy for increasing community support is to raise community expectations. Community support and engagement forces a dialogue on the library, and people who are vested have opinions and ideas. The challenge to large libraries is how to create connections with these individuals and communities within the large city or university. In the world of public libraries, a lesson quickly learned by any new city librarian or mayor is that citizens love their branch libraries. On one hand, they see the need for a large main library, but they do not *feel* it the same way they do for their branch library. In order to sell the idea of a New Main Library in San

Francisco, it became necessary to break it down into programs that people will invest in–the concept of centers based on communities and programs. SFPL has started to move away from academic departments of history, literature, etc., into program-centered collections and access with support from affinity groups, and this will be fully realized in the New Main Library.

The CEII is not just the wires and the "last mile." It is the partnerships and planning of all local organizations interested in bringing together the resources and technology for providing information available through networks and vendors into a locally accessible format. It is the planning, organization and sharing of information content of local interest. As the metaphor for the NII is the "superhighway," the metaphor for the CEII should include on- and off-ramps, city streets, and county roads.

STEPS BEING TAKEN AT SFPL

The San Francisco Public Library is building a $140 million New Main Library, renovating nearly all of its 26 branch libraries, and is reaching toward the goal of being the electronic network hub for public access to information and knowledge in the region. The New Main Library is designed to be the real and virtual community center of the City of San Francisco. It will contain an auditorium and a conference center, an audio and video studio for broadcasting from the library, and a computer network that will connect all branch libraries with the New Main. This building will be the intellectual, cultural, and information hub for the entire community. It will also be connected to the Internet, which will provide access for the user at home, the school, or the office. The community needs local electronic streets for local traffic and on/off ramps to the electronic information highway, and SFPL plans to be a part of that local infrastructure.

The New Main, now under construction for opening in early 1996, will be wired with over 600 multi-media, multi-lingual workstations. SFPL has just been awarded a grant to upgrade the computer system and to purchase the initial multi-media workstations. These workstations will provide access to the online catalog in all languages contained in the library (44 at this time) and include the general indexes to most of the journals in the collection. The workstations will connect directly into the Internet and provide electronic document delivery from the library. A goal of SFPL is to have electronic connection to every home, school, and office in San Francisco by the year 2000 and for the connection to provide for multi-media and multi-lingual capability. In addition, SFPL intends to provide the gateway for the entire community to be connected to the Internet.

In the New Main, there will be centers for patrons with special needs, including The Center for the Deaf and Hearing Impaired and the Center for the Blind and Visually Impaired as well as the Program for Learning Differences. In the Center for the Deaf and Hearing Impaired there will be a collection of closed-captioned videos and specially designed video carrels; an adjacent conference room will have a large screen monitor and amplification devices. TDDs will be available in the Center and at public telephones throughout the library. Patrons with vision impairments will be able to find their way through the Library by means of talking signs activated by infrared transmitters carried by the patron. The Center for the Blind and Visually Impaired will be equipped with high technology devices for information processing, text scanners, voice synthesizers, and other assisted reading devices. The library will be a key institution for building bridges for individuals and groups among local and larger communities and will allow those with special needs to participate in the larger collection of library resources and services. Building on our success of the programs for people with vision and hearing disabilities, SFPL is creating eight centers in the New Main with affiliate support groups as well as some programmatic centers needed by the community. The affinity centers are African-American, Children's, Chinese Cultural, Environmental, Filipino-American, Gay/Lesbian, Learning Differences, and the Latin Interest Collection.

The Telephone Information Program (TIP) project calls for upgrading the telephone system in the branch libraries to allow hotline access for all branches to the Telephone Information and Reference Center. This strategy allows us to concentrate staff with linguistic capability (Chinese, Japanese, Korean, Spanish, and Tagalog) and specialized customer service skills at one central location for the entire city. We will be completing the installation of over 35 dial-up access points to the San Francisco Connection (which consists of the online public access catalog, the community resource files, the online databases from commercial vendors and the connection of the entire system to the National Research and Education Network). Centralized telephone information service will provide service to patrons who cannot physically come to the library and will improve and expand information service to people who currently get busy signals and must call back for an available line. Establishing a twelve-hour daily telephone information service, six days per week, the library will be able to provide the public with simple general information and detailed information about the libraries' holdings and services. This extended service will also assist the public in getting more sophisticated information from the library by reserving the use of the certified librarians for higher level reference work both over the phone and in person.

The TIP program is part of a larger program at San Francisco Public Library, called ACCESS/SFPL. It is a program for increasing access to the library's resources and using those resources in the most effective *and* cost-effective manner possible. There will be Centralized Information and Reference Services including the TIP program, and we will create community resource files to support the work of the paraprofessionals in the Telephone Information and Reference Center. Integral to the success of TIP and ACCESS/SFPL are marketing, promotion, and training in use of the multimedia, multi-lingual workstations. We plan to target schools and community groups with roving trainers and continuing support.

As a part of the ACCESS/SFPL program, we are moving to redefine the roles of our branches as a two-tiered system of Neighborhood Branches and Resource Branches. The Neighborhood Branches will have Children and Youth services with an on-site librarian, circulation services (including adults), Senior Services, and Recreational Reading (which will be managed by Resource Branch and staffed by volunteers). We plan to upgrade Resource Branches; all services available at the Neighborhood Branches will be in the Resource Branches with the addition of Young Adult Programs. Managers for Senior Services and Recreational Reading will be stationed at Resource Branches. At all branches there will be remote information and reference service with an upgraded telephone system and direct access to centralized services.

We plan to provide for remote access to available networks and information resources. There will be a process during which we develop access protocols and policies and negotiate access with vendors. We plan to develop partnerships and purchasing and management collaborations with the local school district and institutions of higher learning. Future parts of the ACCESS/SFPL program might include Safe Haven and Friends for Life. Safe Haven will be a program in which we enlist the help of the Police Department to provide neighborhood Safe Centers in the branches. Friends for Life will be working to deliver library materials to the homebound.

SFPL is using computer hardware from The Digital Equipment Corporation (DEC). The configuration consists of two DEC VAX 6610 processors with 384 megabytes of main memory and 20 gigabytes of disk storage. At this time, the network has over 500 terminals and PCs connected via terminal servers. Users connected via PC are running software that enables the PC to act as a terminal. The dial-up portion of the network consists of two terminal servers with a total of 16 ports. A single telephone number connects users to the first available port. The ports support modems with speeds of up to 9600 bits per second. Dial-in users must have communications software with support for DEC VT terminal emulation. SFPL plans to upgrade the computer hardware to the DEC ALPHA series processors within the next two years. The final configuration has not yet been confirmed, but will most likely include two ALPHA 7000 class processors and another 20 gigabytes of disk storage. A fast, high-density backup device will be needed to accommodate the extra storage capacity. SFPL plans to utilize emerging communications technology that will permit data and images to move at high speeds across the network.

SOLUTIONS

In order to use these strategies to meet the challenges, the library and its staff will have to redefine their roles so as to include and prioritize resources for the new model of service. The library as an organization will have to address the importance of organizing library resources for access with OPACS, inventory, and indexes. The library's mission will need to embrace organization of networked access including the necessity of designing and providing navigation tools, negotiating access rights, providing technology for have-nots, arranging payment for copyright royalties, and providing subsidized access. The library must designate itself as a communications center for the community and as a network hub.

In order to take advantage of the opportunities that are presented to us with the challenges above described, the library profession will need to continue to shift from the role of information gatekeeper to that of information navigator. Librarians will need to acquire and refine skills for the new paradigm. Our skills in the age of printed text and scarcity were selection, acquisition, cataloging, processing, readers' advisory, reference and planning. In blunt terms, the staff will have to shift from being retrievers (getting the book or answer for the patron) to facilitators (designing the system to acquire, organize and connect patrons to the book or answer). We as a profession will need to be proficient at system design and integration; database creation; format selection; and content storage, retrieval and delivery. *All librarians will need to become managers.*

Libraries must work together, with their communities, and with other agencies and institutions to harness the power of the new technologies and help the information or knowledge seeker navigate the scattered information and knowledge resources. This technology has the power to alter the way people live, work, and think. The public library can be the facilitator and the leader locally in this effort. Information resources come from a wide variety of sources both public and private. Those entities involved in the provision of information include libraries of all descriptions, cable tv, telephone and telecom providers, educational institutions, the traditional news media, and information and referral services. There are even static spaces controlled by government or commercial entities, including mass transit boards, electronic kiosks at hotels and airports that can be relevant to and useful for the broader dissemination of community information. Partnerships must be created and maintained and responsibilities defined and assigned so that the greatest number of resources are available to the greatest number of people.

The technology for networking already exists, but there is still much to do to make a Community Electronic Information Infrastructure a reality in the nation's cities and counties. What is necessary is collaboration on a grand scale. The future value of long-established coalitions and cooperatives will not necessarily be the electronic networks, but rather the organizational structures. The hope for the future is collaboration, not confrontation. With the increased access that emerging technologies provide, libraries can help build the organizations needed to bring about the NII and CEII.

CONCLUSION

Change has always been a factor in human history, but the increasing pressures on our communities and institutions is due to the rapidity of change today and the massive scale involved. In the past, the goal of management had been to create predictable futures for their organizations. As we have seen, the rapid changes in society and technology have nullified that model. We must understand that we can no longer plan our organizations based on predictable futures. The management of libraries must understand that resisting change as necessitated by societal changes imperils the institution and the jobs of those within it. By providing leadership through visioning, partnering with other organizations, and developing affinity groups, we can build a Community Electronic Information Infrastructure which will foster healthy libraries and healthy communities.

Information Services
and Economic Development:
New Opportunities for Collaboration

John Haak
Helen B. Josephine
Glenn Miyataki

INTRODUCTION

Economic development is often prescribed as a remedy for many economic and social conditions. Customary objectives of economic development are: to foster growth in various sectors of the economy, expand quality employment opportunities, and improve the well being of the people while maintaining a life-supporting environment.

As all sectors of the community, public as well as private, look for ways to achieve positive economic development, they enter into the challenging and uncertain realm of forecasting the future, finding and mixing just the right ingredients to achieve success. Identi-

John Haak is University Librarian at the University of Hawai'i at Manoa, Honolulu, HI. Helen B. Josephine is Associate Director, Office of Technology Transfer and Economic Development, and Administrator at the University of Hawai'i at Manoa, Honolulu, HI. Glenn Miyataki is Associate Professor, International Management, College of Business Administration at the University of Hawai'i at Manoa, Honolulu, HI.

[Haworth co-indexing entry note]: "Information Services and Economic Development: New Opportunities for Collaboration." Haak, John, Helen B. Josephine, and Glenn Miyataki. Co-published simultaneously in *Journal of Library Administration* (The Haworth Press, Inc.) Vol. 20, Nos. 3/4, 1995, pp. 57-79; and: *The Future of Information Services* (ed: Virginia Steel, and C. Brigid Welch) The Haworth Press, Inc., 1995, pp. 57-79. Multiple copies of this article/chapter may be purchased from The Haworth Document Delivery Center [1-800-3-HAWORTH; 9:00 a.m. - 5:00 p.m. (EST)].

fying trends, defining objectives, choosing strategies, building coalitions and consensus, and selecting specific measures–all enter into the process that eventually leads to an agenda for action. The role of planning in putting together the ingredients of the recipe for success is an important vehicle for implementation as well. This paper will discuss the economic development initiatives in the State of Hawai'i intended to foster the growth of the information industry statewide.

In 1987, the State of Hawai'i began to chart the course for its economic future. The conditions were ripe: a new governor and state administration; a large surplus in the state treasury that could be allocated for investment; widespread recognition that the State's economy needed to diversify beyond the boundaries of its traditional dependencies on tourism, federal military expenditures, and large-scale plantation-based agriculture of sugar and pineapple. It was also recognized that Hawai'i needed to become a more active player in international business and trade markets. The prospects for development that came to the forefront included: stimulating an information services sector within the economy, building a spaceport, harnessing geothermal energy, and implementing high technology initiatives such as the establishment of technical research parks on the islands of Maui, Oahu and Hawai'i. This paper will concentrate on the State's efforts to grow the information services sector.

In the spring of 1987 the Hawai'i State Senate passed a resolution which resulted in a proclamation by Governor John Waihee declaring 1988, "The Year of Telecommunication in the State of Hawai'i." The governor further responded to this resolution by sponsoring a conference in the fall of 1987 for business, government, and educational leaders. The purpose of this conference was to consider ways the State could foster and assist in the growth of information and telecommunications services in Hawai'i. Hawai'i's senior Senator, Daniel K. Inouye, stated that, "telecommunications is more than an infrastructure: it is the heart of every developed economy on the planet." He challenged the assembled to act quickly and take specific steps so Hawai'i could develop a leadership role in the telecommunications economy expanding throughout the Pacific Basin (Governor's Symposium, pp. 137, 139).

Following the conference, the Legislature sprang into action. It formed a number of working groups which developed position papers serving as the basis for legislative hearings. The 1988 Session of the Legislature then passed a series of acts designed to support the development of an information industry in Hawai'i.

The issues faced by the working groups and the Legislature generated a number of key questions: what is an information industry, what are the conditions supportive of growth in an information industry and what should be done now? In their search for answers, the working groups looked at the online information services people were using at that time. Investigations revealed that the university libraries and academic computing centers were the most advanced users and providers of information technology services such as access to databases, file transfers, and electronic mail. At that time almost no private businesses in Hawai'i were engaged in online information services, information processing, or software development. The state was also lacking the computing and telecommunications infrastructure capable of supporting high levels of activity. And there was no government agency in place to encourage and assist public and private participation in the development of an information services industry.

Undaunted by these conditions, the executive and legislative branches of the state government began a series of initiatives to build upon existing strengths and to remedy the conditions of weakness. The Telecommunications and Information Act of 1988 along with following legislation in 1989,[1] appropriated several million dollars and conceptualized a public/private partnership for the creation of services and the development of an appropriate telecommunications infrastructure or gateway(s) and accounting, billing, and collection services for the provision of information services" (Naj and Quirk, p. 3).

Through this legislation a number of information-related economic development initiatives were conceptualized and funded. The State Department of Budget and Finance was given the responsibility to develop and operate the technical infrastructure of the new State of Hawai'i sponsored information gateway and network. The Hawai'i Information Network Corporation (Hawai'i INC), a public entity, was created to encourage the growth of an information industry by enabling private information providers to offer their feebased services via the state's information network, Hawai'i FYI.

The Hawai'i Interactive Television Systems (HITS) operated by the UH Office of Information Technology was funded to provide for statewide distance education. To expand the role of the university library as an information service provider, funding was provided which allowed the library to contract with the CARL Corporation to develop UHCARL, the library's integrated online system and network providing interconnectivity to other libraries in the state as well as those networked by CARL and the Colorado Alliance of Research Libraries. Other units of the University of Hawai'i were charged with establishing a software engineering center, building a university information network to expand the role of the computing center, and developing mechanisms to create and sell access to university controlled data and databases. Through these measures the state began a unified effort to build the technical infrastructure and to develop a set of organizations to manage the infrastructure, create services, and cultivate a market for these services both in the public and the private sector.

Economic development is a complex process and it takes time, especially when the effort is focused upon a new sector of the economy or a new industry. It is not a quick fix and it requires vision as well as fortitude. Each of the institutions in Hawai'i charged with promoting the new information economy have their own stories to tell. This paper will focus on the planning process and the efforts that have been made by the University of Hawai'i Libraries in collaboration with the University's Office of Technology Transfer and Economic Development to create the Library External Services Program.

In order to take advantage of the legislative intent of the development of an information industry infrastructure and the newly authorized ability to create and sell access to University controlled data and databases, the University library embarked on a planning process to discover the viability of a fee-based information service in Hawai'i in support of economic development.

THE STRATEGIC BUSINESS PLANNING PROCESS

The executive and legislative branches provided the political and technological impetus for developing an information industry in Hawai'i. Consequently, the University of Hawai'i was called upon to stimulate economic development through its library resources and networks of libraries throughout the state. In 1989, at least 82 academic library fee-based services were already in operation across the U.S. Although they served as prototypes for the University's effort, none were expected to play a major role in the economic development of their state as the service at the University of Hawai'i was called upon to do. Several major questions pertaining to the viability of an information industry became apparent: Is there a need for such services? Who will use the services? How do we get it started? How do we involve the private sector, both profit and nonprofit organizations? What are the costs and benefits of creating a critical mass in the industry? Will it lead to job creation? Will it add to gross domestic product? The University needed a mechanism for achieving the State's economic vision. New patterns of collaboration were envisioned as well as new potential partnerships that cross traditional organizational boundaries in the public and private sector. New philosophies were needed to guide new methods for delivering library services. All of these became important ingredients for forging an information industry.

A very comprehensive planning process was designed and implemented for addressing the objectives of the enabling legislation. The outcomes of the planning process provided the foundation for the Library External Services Program. The process included a survey of university-wide collections; an analysis of the information needs of business, industry, government, and educational sectors of the State; trends and directions of other fee-based services nationally; identification of key legal issues related to technological considerations; a strategic business plan; and a fee schedule and administrative policy approved by the Board of Regents. The entire planning function began in November 1989 and culminated with approval of the Regents' policy for the new service in March 1992. Important lessons were learned in the process of creating a new entity in the information services industry. Time will confirm whether or not these lessons heightened economic activity in the information industry and encouraged further economic development in the State. The new Library External Services Program began operation in January 1994.

The Supply Side: Information Collections

As a supplier of information, the University needed to identify clearly its potential contribution to the information services industry by surveying the information collections which could potentially be offered through its new information service. The multitude of sources and information collections were ranked by priority and uniqueness based on the anticipated demand for the information. For example, the Hawai'ian and Pacific collections were ranked high, as was the Asian collection, one of the most extensive in the global library community. In addition, the collections from other university campuses such as the Mookini Library on the Big Island of Hawai'i and the Hawai'ian collection from Kauai Community College were included as potentially high-use collections. Finally, collections from other organizations and programs were considered for public use, namely, the East-West Center, Hawai'i Medical Library, Hawai'i Visitors' Bureau, State Legislative Reference Bureau, and County Municipal Records. The extensive network of library resources assured the opportunity for clients to seek information for business and economic purposes from a variety of sources.

The process also envisioned the library's expanded role in facilitating faculty research in the networked environment and improving computer file management to enhance research collaboration via telecommunications. The marketability of full-text electronic research and articles on the Internet is currently a major issue between vendors users and information service providers. As the major brokering agent for information on the "supply" side of the business equation, new opportunities for economic activity can be promoted by the University's assurance that the collections will be current, quickly accessible, and easily retrievable to clients.

Potential Clients and Markets

Any new business opportunity requires the identification of potential clients and markets to target the products and services.

The University used the planning process to launch its market research. A private marketing research firm was contracted to study client needs and unmet demand. Concurrently, a national survey of academic libraries fee-based services was conducted, followed by site visits to five university libraries. The purpose of these studies was to identify the needs of clients, the collections and library services to offer, the markets, the technical infrastructure needed to deliver the products, and the business management practices needed to operate successfully.

The market research revealed many unmet needs for information services which the new service needed to consider. Many organizations using in-house services also indicated that they would use fee-based services at university libraries if they were made available. Online databases were infrequently used by the organizations surveyed. However, they reported that their frequency of use would increase significantly if the University provided access to online databases through its fee-based services program. Popular databases being used in the community were NEXIS/LEXIS, DIALOG, Westlaw, National Library of Medicine, and NewsNet. Other database services which organizations considered using if the University offered them were: Wilsonline, DRI, BRS, and Pergamon (OmniTrak Group, Inc., 1990).

The market research also indicated that government agencies had the greatest awareness of database services. Also, organizations which had more computers and those which anticipated future needs for University library information services had greater awareness of database services. The greatest potential users were generally identified as those larger organizations with more than 100 employees and with computers. The study concluded that it would appear that an increased awareness would have a positive effect on the demand for University information services (OmniTrak Group, Inc., 1990).

The nationwide study of academic library fee-based information services was also conducted to determine various facets of starting a fee-based service, trends, and suggestions for improvements. The survey and site visits to five university libraries provided an in-depth review of fee-based services operations as well as a wealth of knowledge and experience for planning Hawai'i's fee-based service. Various planning processes were identified; different funding models were reviewed; accounting, billing, and invoicing models were studied; computer hardware and software configurations were investigated; external and internal public relations efforts were examined; and the levels of services and the client bases were evaluated.

Reviewing these fee-based services provided a benchmark for the University's new Library External Services Program. A self-supporting, cost recovery model of operation with a subsidy from the administration was proposed as the most effective for serving the university campus population and clients outside the university. The fee-based service needed to be operated in accordance with business principles and its personnel were to have business acumen. Leadership was especially critical and the director of a fee-based service was required to establish the operation on one hand, legitimize it on-campus on the other hand, while at the same time drumming up interest and revenues from the corporate sector and providing quality service. The director's required attributes were a high level of energy, hard work, strong marketing and communication skills, business-orientation, and lots of common sense. The director was thought to be the key to the future success of the operation.

The studies helped to determine the supply and demand for a fledgling industry and the various clients and markets identified to be served were as follows:

- Government agencies
- Business and industry
- Community groups
- Professional associations
- Military personnel
- Professionals/scientists
- Faculty and students
- International/national information centers and libraries
- Consultants, Attorneys, Accountants
- Health services providers
- Individuals

The Strategic Business Plan

The single, most essential document which reflected the planning results was the strategic business plan. It put into words the thoughts, ideas, trends, issues, and decisions which surfaced during the planning process. The strategic plan proposed the mission of the library fee-based service and its core values, the organizational structure, staffing plan, market plan, facilities plan, and a pro forma financial plan. The financial and capitalization plan indicated that with a self-support, cost-recovery model subsidized somewhat by university administration for the first three years of operation, a fee-based service could survive on its own.

The strategic business plan provided the specifications for operating a fee-based library service. Through such a service, the academic library could pursue new opportunities and become partners with off-campus users of information. Highlights of the Library External Services Program as planned were as follows:

1. The program would offer information services to users of library resources: document delivery, loans of books and audio-visual material, custom research using online databases, source verification, translation services, and training for online database and information research.
2. The information resources would be obtained from the specialized collections of the major University library and other database network services and fee-based external service programs in other states.
3. The program would be directed toward the external community who have a need for library services information. The services would be designed to promote and support Hawai'i's economic development and emerging role in the Pacific Basin and Asia with primary markets in business and industry, government agencies, professional associations, educational institutions, and other academic library services.
4. The new fee-based service would provide the training for users to become skilled and discriminating users of new information sources. The growth of online and CD-ROM databases has created interest among users, but they are not always equipped with the necessary skills to fully utilize these sources. The advent and rapid growth of optical scanners and computerized illustrations along with hypertext capabilities

will create new information resources in libraries and on networks that will attract new users.

The essence of this new opportunity is embodied in the mission statement, the core values of the program, and a 5-year market "cultivation" strategy. The mission of the library external services program is:

> To advance the utilization of knowledge by providing the highest quality library information services to organizations and individuals in the business, education, government, and community sectors. (Administrative Policy, p. 4)

Along with this mission, the core values of the program are to serve the clients first with speed, accuracy, and consistency; with an image of pride and professionalism; and with the highest quality of service to the Hawai'i community. As the program matures, it will extend its services to become a major information resource in the Pacific Basin and Asia.

Finally, the success of the program will depend heavily on the ability to "cultivate" clients to use the services. Potential clients and markets need to be identified and direct face-to-face efforts need to be enlisted to educate, train, and illustrate the use of the various services and information collections. Also, partnerships will need to be cultivated with other external academic or educational organizations interested in becoming service providers of their own collections for access and utilization by users of the Library External Services Program. Cultivation will require diligent marketing and a participative process for implementing the program. Housing the service in the University library places it in the arena which reaches learners and researchers of all ages.

Legal Issues

The information industry is considered by many to be the economic foundation of the "post-industrial" society. Products include not only reports, analyses, and data, but also the software that provides the "smarts" in manufactured goods from integrated circuits to automobiles to coffee makers. Business, research, and educational institutions will rely increasingly on telecommunication networks and information services to obtain and maintain competitive advantage. For example, an increasing number of industries will begin to use electronic document interchange, a form of electronic mail in which purchase orders, shipping documents, payments, and other transactions are transmitted electronically without confirmation by paper documents. The development of the information industry will be shaped by the legal issues and organizational responses to technological advancement.

An important part of the planning process for the new library information service was examination of the legal issues related to the information industry. Very little law exists concerning information services, service providers, and the liabilities of the various parties to electronic transactions. Most of the law of information services relies on private contracts, except for federal law concerning intellectual property and private electronic mail and various federal and state computer crime statutes. Thus, opportunities to engage in information services currently provide an undesirable legal environment for doing business for all parties; more certainty is needed concerning the duties and liabilities of parties supplying and using information services. Furthermore, the requirement of having a separate written contract with each user of an information service has the potential of greatly increasing administrative costs and prevents unanticipated or ad hoc uses of information.

The planning process was further designed to anticipate the legal environment in which the information service was intended to prosper. One of the state's top lawyers in technology law was hired to identify the legal issues, address their implications for information services, and make recommendations on how to handle the issues in each category of technology law. The key legal issues resulting from the study and their primary concerns were:

1. Contractual issues regarding the enforceability of electronic contracts and corrupted transactions such as incomplete, inaccurate, or undelivered documents due to transmission or computational defects.
2. Copyright issues on ownership of electronic files and messages, reproducibility of electronic documents to users, own-

ership of value added data to original copyrighted documents, and payment of royalties on duplicated copies.

3. Tort issues, including defamation, fraud, and other wrongful civil transactions perpetrated via information services such as chain letters and pyramid schemes.

4. Product and service liability issues for a defective product or service and implied warranties.

5. Privacy issues regarding the safeguarding of private files and liabilities for misdelivery to the wrong party.

6. Unlicensed practice issues regarding advice found in legal, medical, or other professional information services or bulletin boards.

7. Criminal acts by users for illegal activity such as posting stolen credit card numbers or pirated software.

8. Censorship and sanctions on users regarding liability for objectionable or obscene material accessed through the Library External Services Program.

9. Competition by a state agency with private businesses with regard to pricing, unfair competition, and government subsidies.

Issues of liability were important considerations for creating the legal environment conducive to fostering the growth of the information services industry. Unless these were addressed and precedent known, the adhocracy of dealing with legal issues may expose parties to inconsistent and unenforceable policies and practices. One of the key underlying elements of effective collaboration needs to rely upon the legal integrity of the partnership.

Implementation of the Strategic Business Plan

The approval of the strategic business plan in January 1990 triggered the process for developing the necessary Board of Regents policy and State of Hawai'i Administrative Rules for implementation of the program. The legitimation process for implementing the strategic business plan required extensive and intensive participation from faculty, staff, and administration of all of the campuses of the University system. In addition, librarians statewide and several professional associations were provided a preview of the concept of the new fee-based program and were invited to comment on its development. The development of the Board of Regents policy and the companion Executive policy for administrative execution were essentially in-house approval processes. The process provided the opportunity to increase the awareness and understanding of the Library External Services Program and to address implementation concerns of the university community. Some of the common issues raised were:

1. What is the relationship between the regular library program, access to the Library External Services program, and the charging of fees for services which have been customarily free on some campuses and not others?
2. What are the costs vs. benefits of a campus operating its own external services program and what kind of resource support can the campus expect from the university system administration?
3. What is the relationship between the fees to be charged by the Library External Services Program and fees already charged by each campus in for instance the campus outreach programs, the computer center, and the office of instructional support?
4. What is the relationship between the regular library staff and the external services program staff and how will the regular library program staff be compensated for assistance provided to the fee-based service?
5. How will the campus justify the issue of unfair competition by commercial entities which may have a close tie to a campus?
6. How will the interlibrary loan process be handled to be equitable and fair to all of the campuses?

The policy development process provided an immense opportunity to the university community for input and feedback on these issues. Several important "messages" were learned in the process which served as a lesson of the power of participation and overcoming resistance in the pursuit of innovation and change. One of the most important messages was to ensure that the library needs of faculty, students, and staff remain primary and not compete with the external services program for library materials. Furthermore, the geographic distances and physical isolation of campuses on the neighbor islands raised the issue of equitable treatment with regard to access to the system and the payment of fees for services. Finally, rapid technological advancements in library hardware and software systems were changing the meaning and application of customary library services, softening the distinction between traditional services which were free and external services which were for fee. The primary concern reemphasized the philosophy that the library exists for both off and on-campus faculty, students, and staff and their usage must continue to be preserved at all costs, including subsidies to provide an equitable and level playing field.

The development of the State of Hawai'i Administrative Rules encompassing the fee schedule for the new service provided the general public with the opportunity to participate. Through public hearings held on the islands of the state, the general public was provided an opportunity to review and comment on the fee structure and services to be offered by the program. Concerns expressed during the hearings were considered in the development of the Board of Regents policy and the Hawai'i Administrative Rules. The right to public input was another ingredient for ensuring the potential success of the new information service.

In summary, the comprehensive planning process was very helpful in forging promising opportunities for collaboration in the developing information industry. The services developed through these efforts will attract an increasing number of users because of staff time saved in research, the effectiveness of the service to deliver accurate and relevant information sources and material, and the accessibility and retrievability of information from almost anywhere. Prices or fees for such services were not found to be an obstacle because of the relative price inelasticity of desirable information services. The market survey showed that demand was strong enough that behavior in using such information services would not be driven solely by price. More important than price was the quality, timeliness, and accuracy of the information (OmniTrak Group, Inc., 1990). The Library External Services Program has the potential to provide the University of Hawai'i with another avenue to further relationships and promote partnerships in the advancement of knowledge, technology, humanity, and business and economic development.

OPERATION OF THE LIBRARY
EXTERNAL SERVICES PROGRAM

The structure of the current library External Services Program is very different from other similar services found in academic libraries. First, as described above, start-up funds were from the state legislature as part of a larger initiative to develop information services and industries in Hawai'i. Second, administration of the service reports to both the University Librarian at the University of Hawaii and the Director of the Office of Technology Transfer and Economic Development for the University of Hawai'i. Third, other University of Hawai'i departments and organizational units with information services or products are encouraged to be part of the Library External Services Program as service providers to strengthen the overall information offerings of the University of Hawai'i in support of economic development.

Funds for the development of a fee-based information service and the University of Hawai'i information network authorized by the passage of The Telecommunications and Information Act of 1988 were placed in a revolving fund administered by the economic development arm of the University, the Office of Technology Transfer and Economic Development. These funds were used "to create the capacity to access information resources in other research libraries; to expand high speed communication links among University libraries and computing centers; to link University libraries to local, regional, national, and international databases; to convert University libraries' card catalogs and information files to machine readable form; and to develop the necessary mechanism to package and sell University controlled data and databases" (Act 1 SpSLH, Section 14). Within the library the funds were used to contract with the CARL Corporation to develop the UHCARL system which allowed the library to network with other research libraries as well as to develop a state-wide University of Hawai'i library network. Additional funds were set aside for the development of a program to provide university library-based information services on a fee basis as part of the development of an information industry in the state of Hawai'i.

The Office of Technology Transfer and Economic Development

was designated to provide university-wide administrative oversight of the expenditure of the funds for the development of the UHCARL System and the Library External Services Program. However, no funds were allowed to be expended for the new service until a business plan was developed and approved. The strategic business plan (1989-1990) and the planning process helped the Library and the Office of Technology Transfer and Economic Development determine what services could be developed and offered on a cost recovery basis. Finally in 1992 the development and approval of the University of Hawai'i Administrative Rules and Policies gave the new service the authority to charge for certain types of services. Responding to concerns raised in public hearings that traditional library services would only be offered on a fee basis, the policy explicitly states that "this program in not intended to be a substitute for traditional library services that must continue to be offered freely to all UH faculty, students, and staff" (Administrative Policy, p. 2).

Based on the results of the surveys and interviews conducted by the strategic business plan consultants, a list of possible services was developed and is included in the Administrative Policy. These library information services are interpreted broadly to include "those services that pertain to the creation, production, or dissemination of information collections and technologies that are held, controlled, or licensed by a University of Hawai'i campus library or organizational unit" (Administrative Policy, p. 2).

The initial services offered directly by the program include document and text retrieval and delivery, research services, and training sessions to help people become confident users of information networks and services. Clients external to the University of Hawai'i have been defined to include all library users outside the UH system such as businesses, government agencies, educational institutions, libraries, professional organizations, community groups, and individuals. Organizationally within the University of Hawai'i library, the traditional Interlibrary Loan department has been changed to reflect the emergence of the new service. Interlibrary Loan at the University of Hawai'i has been restructured to handle all requests from University of Hawai'i faculty and students for material not held at the University of Hawai'i Manoa campus as well as all requests from the University of Hawai'i community college libraries, the University of Hawai'i Hilo Library and the University of Hawai'i West Oahu Library for material held at the Manoa Campus. All other requests for material from the University of Hawai'i at Manoa will be filled and billed by the Library External Services Program.

In addition to these core services, the Library External Services Program is establishing service centers in collaboration with three other university information-related organizational units outside the library. The Administrative Policy allows for the development of information services by other University of Hawai'i campus units or organizational units as service centers tied to the Library External Services Program with a mutually-agreed operational configuration. The first adjunct service will be provided by the College of Language, Linguistics, and Literature through its Language Telecommunications Resource and Learning Center. The Center will offer community and business organizations access to satellite earth station down links and uplinks for video and audio satellite transmissions as well as producing copies of language instruction audio tapes developed by University of Hawai'i faculty.

The second service center currently in place is with the Hawai'i Interactive Television Service (HITS) operated by the University's Office of Information Technology. This service extends the five interactive television classroom sites on four islands to other public agencies and businesses who wish to view a university class, participate in interactive teleconferencing between the islands or throughout Asia and the Pacific through the HITS connection to the satellite links provided by the Language Telecommunications Resource and Learning Center.

The third service under development is with the College of Business Administration. This service will provide community and business access to the Electronic Meeting Room housed in the College of Business Administration. This facility was originally developed for faculty research in the use of decision-making software or groupware. Under the terms of the software license, community and business groups can use the facility with the assistance of facilitators from the College of Business. By providing this service in conjunction with the Library External Services Program, the business community can have access to the latest information relating to their business decisions as well as access to a state-of-the art facility to help make those decisions.

Together these service centers and the core services of research and document delivery provide the business and professional community with a complementary set of information support services designed to help users adapt to the information age, equalize access to information throughout the islands, and provide timely access to information needed for economic development.

The development of the UHCARL System as part of the information infrastructure of the state includes access to the online catalogs and locally-produced databases of the University of Hawai'i at Manoa Library as well as access to the University of Hawaii at Hilo, Kapiolani Community College, Maui Community College, Kauai Community College and the University of Hawai'i at Manoa School of Law Library. During the first quarter of 1994, the University of Hawai'i, West Oahu campus and Leeward Community College will be added to the UHCARL system. Access to UHCARL is available state-wide via dial-in ports, Hawai'i F, the state's information network, and terminals located in public and school libraries. Requests for book loans, photocopies, and research from users not affiliated with the UH System are referred to the Library External Services Program.

Through its link with the University of Hawai'i systemwide Office of Technology Transfer and Economic Development, the Library External Services Program will participate fully in the activities of the Intellectual Property Program, the Economic Development and Education Program, the Technical Assistance Program, and the University Seed Capital Program. All of these programs are designed to facilitate the many aspects of the transfer of university-based research into the private sector to further the economic development of the state. As an integral part of this effort, the Library External Services Program will provide online research and document delivery to the other programs in the Office of Technology Transfer and Economic Development as well as participate in conferences and projects jointly sponsored by the Small Business Administration, the State of Hawai'i Department of Economic Development and Tourism, the Research Corporation of the University of Hawai'i, and the Pacific International Center for High

Technology Research. These relationships will build the collaborative foundation needed to sustain an information industry in Hawai'i.

The policy governing the Library External Services Program also allows for the development of collaborative efforts outside of the University provided that "the information collection of the provider is consistent with the priority program areas identified in the University of Hawai'i plans and budgets and will therefore enhance the University's information services . . . [and] . . . the information collection has redeeming value and reflects the unique advantages of Hawai'i's cultural, ecological, geographical, and international business orientations to Asia and the Pacific Basin" (Administrative Policy, pp. 7-8).

The Library External Services Program is actively seeking partnerships and opportunities with other state agencies and business groups to develop information offerings consistent with this policy. Since 1991 UHCARL has been an information service provider on Hawai'i FYI, the state-wide electronic services gateway developed by Hawai'i INC. Further collaborative efforts by the Library External Services Program and Hawai'i INC are planned such as joint marketing and end-user training as well as additional database offerings and automated ordering of documents.

The governing policy also allows institutions external to the University to contract through the Library External Services Program for automated library services and access to UHCARL. In January 1993, the Bernice Pauahi Bishop Museum Archives/Library was added to the UHCARL System. The addition of this library and the Hawai'i Medical Library in 1992 further enhances the potential information offerings of the Library External Services Program. Negotiations are underway to add additional unique private research collections as funding becomes available.

CONCLUSION

The institutions of our culture called libraries embody values, traditions, processes, and resources which preserve and transmit our heritage of information, knowledge, and experience. Research libraries have been built over time to support parent institutions' academic programs, faculty, and students. With the new-found power to communicate information and to provide services through the utilization of information technologies and evolving networks, research libraries now have the opportunity to extend their value not only to their traditional clientele but also to other communities including business and professional communities. Through this process of extension, along with changing philosophies and perceptions toward access, research libraries hold the possibility of increasing their utility, diversifying their base of financial support, and evolving as instruments of service within the new world information culture.

The libraries of the University of Hawai'i are following this vision of extension supported by the economic development initiatives of the State. There has been statewide recognition that the University Library resources are a statewide asset, not a liability. The Library of the University of Hawai'i at Manoa has benefitted substantially. Its technological infrastructure has been upgraded, and services have been enhanced through the Library's partnership with the CARL Corporation. These two organizations hold a common view for the future of libraries in the networked environment, one that embraces the intentions of the legislation passed in Hawai'i in 1988. The library staff have also become competent developers, users, and instructors of new information tools and services. And the Library External Services Program has moved through its rites of passage to the stage of implementation.

The libraries of the other campuses of the University, the Bishop Museum, and the Hawai'i Medical Library have also benefitted. By joining the UHCARL system they have been able to automate their services at a fraction of the cost of a stand-alone system, and they gain the power, as well, that comes with participating in the networked environment with access to the wide array of information resources provided through the CARL network.

People benefit. The holdings of the libraries utilizing the UHCARL system may be identified through a variety of networks including the CARL Network, the Internet, and Hawai'i FYI, the Hawai'i state network managed by Hawai'i INC. An individual may utilize the databases and services provided through the UHCARL system from any of the 49 libraries comprising the State Public Library

System, from any one of the 238 public schools, and from the ten campuses of the University of Hawai'i. Any person in the State of Hawai'i may dial-in to the UHCARL system with a local telephone call.

One of the goals of the information initiative of the state government has been to improve access to resources held in university libraries. Use of the UHCARL system is very high on the state network and is growing at a rapid pace in terms of number of users, database selects, and time on the system. The number of connects per month into the UHCARL database consistently ranks in the top 10 of the 90 services offered via Hawai'i FYI. Total UHCARL connect minutes have risen dramatically from 8,718 minutes in July 1992 to 28,187 minutes in July 1993. The libraries of the University have played a positive role in attracting growing numbers of citizens to the information services provided through the state network.

The major goal of expanding the state economy by growing a local information industry remains to be realized. Collaborative efforts spearheaded by the new Library External Services Program will unite the information offerings of the various units and departments of the University, assist the statewide economic development efforts of the University and various state agencies, and extend the resources of the University Library to users in all communities throughout the world. The challenge for the new service is to attract customers to a set of information services and to increase the general understanding of the role information plays in the quality of life in Hawai'i. This new venture is being closely watched not only by government, but also by private interests who are waiting to see how a market for such services might develop before committing their own capital to such an adventure.

TIMELINE

1987   Resolution passed declaring 1988 "The Year of Telecommunication in Hawai'i."

1988   Governor's Symposium on Telecommunications Now and in the Future, Kaanapali, Hawai'i.

Governor's Congress on Hawai'i's International Role, Honolulu, Hawai'i.

1988   Telecommunications and Information Act (Act 1 SpSLH 1988) Funds appropriated for the development of the University of Hawai'i Information Network, and the State of Hawai'i Information Network Corporation.

1989-90   Strategic Business Plan for the Library External Services Program developed and transmitted to the Hawai'i State legislature.

1990   Legislative Management Act (Act 347 SLH 1990).

          Funds appropriated for the installation of public access terminals in schools and school libraries, in the libraries of the Hawai'i State Public Library System, in all libraries of the University of Hawai'i System including the Richardson School of Law and the community colleges, in all court libraries, and in all state office buildings.

1992   Hearings held by the University of Hawai'i Board of Regents on the islands of Kauai and Oahu for public comment on the proposed fee schedule for the Library External Services Program.

1992   Administrative Policy approved as University of Hawai'i, Executive Policy, E2.208.

          Fee Structure approved as University of Hawai'i System-wide Administrative Policy, A 6.100 and Hawai'i Administrative Rules, Title 20 Chapter 21.

1993   Administrator of the Library External Services Program hired.

1994   Library External Services Program begins operation.

REFERENCES

Darby, George E. "Hawaii, the Information Industry and Economic Development," *Pacific Telecommunication Connectivity: Users. Networks and Information Services: Proceedings of the 11th Pacific Telecommunications Conference* (1989: Honolulu, Hawai'i).

Lassner, David. "Overview and Current Progress of the Hawai'i FYI Videotex Project," *International Symposium on Videotex Development in the Asia Pacific* (June 22-24, 1993: Singapore).

Naj, Lindy. "The CARL System at the University of Hawai'i UHM Library," *Library Software Review* 12:1 Spring 1993 pp. 5-11.

Naj, Lindy and Ruth Marie Quirk. "Creating an Information Industry in Hawai'i: The State Government's Pro-Active Approach and Its Potential for Success," *Proceedings of the 8th International Telecommunications Society Conference* (1990: Venice, Italy).

Newcombe, Tod. "Hawai'i FYI: A Working Model for Tomorrow," *Government Technology* 6:5 May 1993 pp. 1, 60, 64.

OmniTrack Group, Inc. *University of Hawai'i Library Information System Survey* (prepared under contract to GKM Associates, Honolulu, 1990).

Proceedings–Governor's Symposium on High Technology (1987: Kaanapali, Maui). Honolulu: High Technology Development Corporation, 1988.

State of Hawai'i, Fourteenth Legislature, 1988, Act 1, "Relating to Telecommunications and Information (Act 1, SpSLH, 1988).

Strategic Business Plan for a Library External Services Program. University of Hawaii at Manoa (1990: GKM Associates, Honolulu).

University of Hawai'i. Executive Policy–Administration, E2.208, August 1, 1992.

University of Hawai'i. System-wide Administrative Policy, A6.100, March 16, 1992.

International and Foreign Information Services in the Expanding Global Community

Paul Zarins

As one information consultant has written, " . . . just because you need to think and act globally doesn't necessarily mean that you're going to have an easy time of it . . . you need to find out about demand, competition, demographics, culture, and economic and legal barriers and regulations. And the commodity that's needed to pull all this off is *information*–a lot of information."[1] In this article I want to review first the growing importance of providing international and foreign information and then look at some of the challenges associated with its provision–challenges shared with information services in general as well as challenges more specific to the international and foreign sphere. Finally, I want to offer some thoughts on approaches to meet these challenges, with particular emphasis on the structures and management of networks of experts.

Paul Zarins is International and Foreign Law Librarian at the National Law Center of the George Washington University, Washington, DC. From 1971 to 1989 he was a librarian at the University of California, San Diego, where his positions included Reference Librarian, Bibliographer for European and United States History, Coordinator of the Computer-Assisted Reference Service, and Government Documents Librarian. He is currently the author of the "What's Online in International Law" column in the *American Society of International Law Newsletter.*

[Haworth co-indexing entry note]: "International and Foreign Information Services in the Expanding Global Community." Zarins, Paul. Co-published simultaneously in *Journal of Library Administration* (The Haworth Press, Inc.) Vol. 20, Nos. 3/4, 1995, pp. 81-96; and: *The Future of Information Services* (ed: Virginia Steel, and C. Brigid Welch) The Haworth Press, Inc., 1995, pp. 81-96. Multiple copies of this article/chapter may be purchased from The Haworth Document Delivery Center [1-800-3-HAWORTH; 9:00 a.m. - 5:00 p.m. (EST)].

Obtaining information from international and foreign sources has become a necessity for many research questions in legal, economic, political, environmental, and other areas. The increasing interdependence of societies and economies is a theme heard almost constantly, although various observers and critics draw disparate conclusions from this growing interdependence. For example, Walter Wriston, the former chief executive of Citibank, in analyzing what he sees as a single global economy, finds that "borders are no longer boundaries; technology has made them porous" with the welcome result that "it is increasingly difficult to keep one's citizens out of the global conversation."[2] Ultimately Wriston sees fundamental, positive changes in the nature of national sovereignty, as the title *The Twilight of Sovereignty* indicates. The critic Wendell Berry, on the other hand, draws pessimistic conclusions from these same developments. "The great, greedy, indifferent national and international economy is killing rural America, just as it is killing American cities–it is killing our country."[3]

The increasing interdependence of societies and economies meshes with another well-established trend–the growing importance of information generally. Information is a prerequisite for knowledge, and as Peter Drucker argues, "knowledge has become the key resource for all work."[4] Regardless of whether Wriston, Berry, or other critics prove to be the most accurate in their analyses and forecasts, one constant in any further debate, analysis, research, and coping strategies is the need for information. Furthermore, these information needs are branching out into more and more subject areas. For example, human rights issues, including the activities of various regional human rights courts and commissions, are receiving increased attention. Intellectual property rights, made more important by technological developments such as computer software, but subject to very different laws among various nations, are also of importance. The challenge of obtaining and analyzing information to produce knowledge about international topics in these and many other subjects is considerable. In the pessimistic view of Wendell Berry, it is an overwhelming task. "Living as we now do in almost complete dependence on a global economy, we are put inevitably into a position of ignorance and irresponsibility. No one can know the whole globe."[5] Berry may be correct to some extent, but the responsibility of libraries is to assist as much as possible the efforts of those who are working to overcome this ignorance about global matters.

Given the dual impetus of increasing internationalization of so many fields and of growing importance of information generally, the question for most libraries is not simply whether or not to provide resources and research consultation for international and foreign sources. The question is to what extent does a particular institution or information service participate in this internationalization of information? To borrow from the terminology of fuzzy logic, decisions about providing information on an international scope will not lead to "crisp sets" of institutions that do or do not need to provide such information. Instead, it is a question of grades of membership or "membership values." "Fuzziness seeps into everything and often appears in surprising places."[6] Fuzziness in decisions about how to deal with international information is not surprising, but finding the best approaches presents a number of challenges.

GENERAL CHALLENGES FOR INFORMATION SERVICES

One such challenge is the growing abundance and even over-abundance of information available from a large variety of sources and the consequent need to locate the most relevant and the best information and present it in a comprehensible package. As McNeill and Freiberger point out in discussing fuzzy logic, "we cut the flood of information down to the trickle we need . . . We perceive the precise in a fuzzy way . . . this ability [is] one of the most important we possess . . . "[7] It is the librarian's task to help make the flood of information from which this trickle is drawn known and accessible, and thus the trickle method, while an answer for library users, is not the solution for our own work. We do need to assist and guide users in making the information understandable, so that they can select what they need. In *Information Anxiety* Richard Wurman points out that "there are only three kinds of businesses that have to do with the dissemination of information: businesses of transmission, storage, and understanding . . . What is virtually untapped is the third component: the understanding business. Understanding is the bridge between data and knowledge."[8] While libraries certainly need experts who understand and apply new developments in the transmission and storage areas, it is the understanding component that offers libraries their most important role to contribute to today's knowledge society. This basic challenge is, of course, not unique to international information, but it is likely to be a particular and continuing challenge on the international front. As Eugene Skolnikoff points out, "the generation of relevant information will increase as global issues proliferate and as technology becomes better able to measure all relevant variables of an issue."[9]

Related to the information flood challenge is another basic question, that of actual ownership of information sources versus provision of access. This too is not a question unique to international information, but once again it is likely to be all the more pressing due to added dispersal of sources and an even greater variety of access methods and protocols. When provision of access instead of local ownership is satisfactory, the further question arises of whether a library or information center is necessary at all. As S. Michael Malinconico has pointed out, "Electronic technologies will make available . . . an enormous richness of information and services without the need to visit traditional libraries . . . Users will be more likely to seek advice from colleagues or technical experts than from librarians or information specialists."[10]

SPECIFIC CHALLENGES FOR INTERNATIONAL INFORMATION SERVICES

In addition to these challenges, which international and foreign information shares with all types of information requests, there are additional problems that are more specific to this area. One continuing barrier is the challenge of identifying, locating, and evaluating translations into a language accessible to the user. English-speaking researchers, often spoiled by the vast amounts of information available in English, are often surprised, disappointed, and possibly impatient when the material they seek does not exist in an English translation. The challenges of language are particularly well demonstrated in foreign law. Translations of needed codes or laws may not exist. If they do exist, close attention must be paid to quality and reliability, particularly since special terminology or usage of words in meanings different from their colloquial context complicates matters. Since official translations are available only infrequently, what is the reliability of unofficial translations? Commercial on-demand services are appearing to fill this demand. One vendor's advertisement promises "a network of highly-regarded foreign law publishers and foreign law firms," with the final result that "information is clear and accurate." These services are needed, but how does one monitor the quality of such on-demand products? (For a discussion of the various hurdles in finding foreign legal materials, including the translation question, see the introduction of the excellent *Foreign Law; Current Sources of Codes and Basic Legislation in Jurisdictions of the World* by Thomas Reynolds and Arturo Flores.)[11]

These translation hurdles are not limited to esoteric materials from smaller nations. The major online service LEXIS, for example, has a library of databases entirely in French. Furthermore, these French files contain not only the expected French national materials, but also international materials such as the texts of decisions from the European Court of Justice, the main court of the European Community. Although these decisions are available in another file in English, delays in translation by the EC mean that in some instances a European Court of Justice decision may initially be available only in French.

Even for materials available in English, differences in terminology can create temporary but unexpected barriers. Locating the First and Second Banking Directives of the European Community provides specific examples of such difficulties. The actual titles of these important directives do not refer to banking. Instead there is the "Second Council Directive 89/646 of 15 December 1989 on the Coordination of Laws, Regulations and Administrative Provisions to the Taking Up and Pursuit of the Business of Credit Institutions and Amending Directive 77/780."[12] One could conceivably be looking at this citation and not realize that the somewhat cryptic title is in fact the required Second Banking Directive. Complicating matters is the problem that some of the first versions of commercially produced CD-ROM databases excluded this particular directive as part of an inexplicable gap in coverage. For a library with sufficient emphasis on EC materials to justify having someone with expertise in EC research, this type of problem presents minimal difficulties. For others, whether they are users doing their own searching or reference librarians without expertise in the area, it can be a frustrating exercise.

Just dealing with the veritable alphabet soup of acronyms and sorting out membership and affiliation questions of international organizations can be a challenging task. The EC (European Community) is not connected with the ECE (Economic Commission for Europe of the United Nations); the European Court of Justice is the highest court of the EC, but the European Court of Human Rights is not affiliated with the EC but rather with the Council of Europe. (The combination of decisions from these two entirely separate courts into one file called ECCASE on the LEXIS online service often adds to the confusion.) Furthermore, almost as if to challenge anew those who have figured out the details of what entities are and are not part of the EC, the well-known European Community itself decided in late 1993 to change its name to the European Union (EU), along with some complementary and confusing name changes for certain subbodies. Another important entity is the CSCE (Conference on Security and Cooperation in Europe), also known popularly as the Helsinki Process, which in the past was not truly an organization. For many years the CSCE was more a process and a series of conferences, although today it finally has a secretariat in Prague and can be viewed as a true organization. There is also a CSCE in Washington, D.C., which is the Commission on Security and Cooperation in Europe, a U.S. commission designed to monitor human rights matters related to the Conference. Suffice it to say that even a moderate dose of all these acronyms and affiliations is a sure recipe for an information headache.

The search for international information is further complicated in that its producers are not limited to governments or well-known world or regional organizations. Eugene Skolnikoff points out that "transnational activities of a large and growing volume are conducted by individuals, groups, and corporations, often outside the direct control or even the knowledge of the state."[13] He goes on to argue the great importance of this internationalized information

outside of state control, for example in such events as the collapse
of the communist governments of Eastern Europe and the Soviet
Union.[14] This plethora of sources obviously adds to the difficulties
in identifying and obtaining the necessary information.

Such complexities may be expected when dealing with questions
that clearly require the use of foreign and international sources. One
might expect clear sailing when it appears that U.S. sources will
provide the necessary information. Unfortunately, there are unexpected barriers here as well. Take the important example of treaties.
Having timely and complete access to the texts of such international
agreements is obviously of considerable importance. Such access
could also be reasonably expected in official sources, at least for
treaties to which the U.S. is a party, since under Article VI of the
U.S. Constitution treaties have the same effect as laws. Unfortunately, by the late 1980s the delay in official publication of treaties
and international executive agreements had fallen as much as five
or more years behind. Librarians addressing this problem found that
by 1989 there was a backlog of at least 2300 treaties and agreements in force but not yet published by the State Department.[15]

My purpose in discussing these specific examples is only to
create an appreciation of the types of difficulties encountered in
information retrieval in the international and foreign arena. As a
final example I want to mention one that demonstrates the relevance
of international information in what would appear to be a purely
domestic issue. One might expect that the finer points of the Inter-
American System of Human Rights, as implemented under the
auspices of the Organization of American States through the Inter-
American Commission on Human Rights and the Inter-American
Court of Human Rights, would be of interest only to researchers
studying human rights violations in Central and South America.
Yet, in 1992 the domestic issue of District of Columbia statehood
took on international aspects when representatives of the Statehood
Solidarity Committee appeared before the Inter-American Commission to argue that the District's lack of statehood constitutes a
human rights violation under international agreements enforced by
the OAS. This effort could not be dismissed as the uninformed
efforts of statehood fanatics, since it was supported by the expertise
of a major law school's international human rights clinic.[16] With

this development, activists, citizens and researchers found a need to understand international law and human rights questions in what had appeared to be only a domestic matter.

ACQUISITIONS AND FORMAT CONSIDERATIONS

Having identified some of the problems encountered in providing international and foreign information, we can turn to the question of what approaches might be used now and in the near future to meet these challenges. To begin with, most information services will need to maintain and to expand access to a core of international and foreign reference sources, even if the primary mission of the service is not focused on this area. Ready access to basic reference works, such as the *Yearbook of International Organizations,* is necessary to make sense of the alphabet soup of organizations.[17] The price of such reference works can be steep, and acquisitions librarians hard pressed to stay within budgetary constraints and to decrease commitments to continuing serials expenditures may be tempted to propose cancellations or to purchase new editions only sporadically. Given the importance of international questions, such measures should come only as a last resort. We can expect an increasing number of these reference sources to be available in CD-ROM and online database formats, and thus the local ownership versus provision of access question will recur frequently.

It is very likely that commercially produced products will increasingly step in to fill the gaps left by official publications. It is still possible that the problem of severe delays in official publications, whether these are the above-mentioned U.S. treaties or other sets from various governments and organizations, will be solved by the application of automation. Limited government and organization funding, however, makes prospects less than bright in most cases. In the case of U.S. treaties commercial publishers are already offering products in online, CD-ROM, microfiche, and paper formats.[18] Another example is the *Yearbook of the United Nations,* the value of which was diminished by publication delays of four to five years. The *Yearbook* is now published by Martinus Nijhoff on behalf of the U.N. Department of Public Information, with some improvement in currency. An important contribution from the ranks of associations is the well-established *International Legal Materials* of the American Society of International Law, a publication that provides on a selective basis unofficial but timely copies of key treaties and other international documents.[19]

Researchers will continue to prefer consulting and citing official sources, but they may be forced to rely increasingly on commercial alternatives for recent materials (with recent defined as perhaps within the last five years). Privatization should in many cases lead to more current and more useful services, but it will also mean increased expenditures for acquisitions. The value of depository arrangements with government and international organizations may diminish. At the same time, commercial products need careful and critical appraisal. For example, some of the new commercial products that have moved to fill the gap on U.S. treaty publications have themselves suffered, at least initially, from delays, gaps, and other problems. As more products from various publishers appear in CD-ROM and online database formats, decisions will need to be made about maintaining paper copies. Paper copies of a good and reasonably-priced product, such as *International Legal Materials,* should be retained even when there is online availability. More difficult are decisions for highly expensive products, products for which online availability is tied to the purchase of another format, and for online databases not available to certain types of accounts, such as academic library users.

ROLE OF THE EXPERT/LIBRARIAN

Although these questions of acquisitions and formats are important, the most important questions are and will be those related to the role of experts, the development of expert networks, and the management of these expert networks. In order to provide access to the wealth of international information and to enhance the understanding of this information, decisions about the role of experts need to be made. A basic question is whether there is sufficient demand in a particular library or information service for one or more experts in particular international subject areas. Furthermore, what is the proper role of such experts within the team of reference librarians and consultants? Peter Drucker argues that "modern organization is an organization of knowledge specialists," and that "unless they know more than anybody else in the organization, they are to all intents and purposes useless."[20] This view might lead to the conclusion that a library needs to have as many experts in specific areas as possible, and that, as much as possible, questions in relevant areas should be directed to these experts. The complexities of international and foreign information access are certainly great enough to argue that it is one area in which such expertise should be maintained, with each institution assessing its degree of membership in this expertise.

On the other hand there is Lewis Perelman's view that "expertise is more in the network, less in the person," and "teamwork via computer-mediated groupware is obliterating the elite role of the personal expert."[21] Accepting Perelman's view might lead to an organization with fewer experts and more emphasis on using the advances of computerized communications to reach experts outside one's own institution.

One model that combines the strengths of the personal expert and the advantages of the network is the "answer network" proposed by Thomas Malone and John Rockart in their discussion of emerging organizational structures. They describe "answer networks" which "would involve massive databases and layers of human experts in many different topic areas."[22] Such "answer networks" have already partially formed through the rapid growth of electronic discussion groups communicating via electronic mail. One example is the INT-LAW discussion group for international law librarians. With INT-LAW, as with many other similar groups, there is already in place a network of experts, encompassing a wide range of subject expertise and far-flung geographical distribution.[23] By January 1994 INT-LAW had grown to 617 participants. While U.S. participants comprised about 70% of the total, it is encouraging that some 29 countries were represented on this list. A comparison of the time, effort, and good luck necessary just a couple of years ago to identify and reach experts with a particular subject proficiency with the current ease of almost instantaneous broadcast of a request to a group of experts is a good measure of the success already accomplished in this networking. We can expect increased participation from more experts from more countries, as well as the formation of many new, specialized discussion groups. Given that United Nations membership had reached over 180 countries by the end of 1993, there is obviously much more work to be done to make a group such as INT-LAW even approach being a global network of experts. Of course, this continuing growth is already creating a new avalanche of information. To prevent disillusionment and a reactive shrinking in participation, automated filtering techniques via software will need to be used more frequently to make most efficient use of multiple expert networks.

RESOURCE SHARING

The importance of resource sharing among institutions is likely to continue to grow. The answer network is not completed by rapid communication among experts and those seeking expert advice. There is still the need for access to the actual information, whether it is in the massive databases referred to by Rockart and Malone, traditional printed sources, or other formats. There is the risk that while communication may be rapid, it will become a frustrating experience of sharing tales of information unavailability. If more and more institutions, including the larger research libraries, come to depend on contacting outside experts and access instead of ownership of resources, users may decide that libraries are an unnecessary detour and turn instead directly to such outside experts. The best situation will be if organizations can maintain the local expertise and resources for particular areas of emphasis, and then the networked teamwork utilizes this expertise for much wider benefit.

Those institutions which do choose to maintain expertise and resources in particular areas must, however, have sufficient incentives and funding to play such a role. Internal funding, secured to support the institution's own teaching and research needs, will probably not allow these institutions to respond fully to the flood of inquiries and requests likely to be generated by the growth of answer networks. There will be an increasing need to establish arrangements for cooperation and resource sharing.

One interesting example of resource sharing is the New York Joint International Law Program consortium, in which three New York law schools with a need to improve international law resources coordinated collection development, expedited document delivery, and the sharing of one international law librarian consultant to serve all three institutions.[24] The inter-institutional sharing of a consultant suggests further that libraries may need to give more serious consideration to the option of regularly allocating funds to purchase outside expertise in areas for which they cannot maintain their own expertise. Fee-based services can offer not only copies of documents but also specialized research expertise, and such expertise could even be offered on a subscription basis to other institutions. Traditional interlibrary loan, with its requests for known, verified items, will prove a satisfactory service in fewer and fewer cases. The mutual help and professional courtesy assistance among colleagues at various institutions will continue, but it can easily overburden the staff and resources of those libraries that have invested in the specialized resources which few others may have. If arrangements, including appropriate monetary compensation, have been made in advance, a system of rapid information delivery that does not take unfair advantage of another institution will be developed.

Building such arrangements for quick access to not only resources but also expertise is one of the major advantages libraries can offer to their users. To quote S. Michael Malinconico again, "we have failed to consider another equally plausible scenario whereby information resources are drawn into the orbits of influence of those who maintain the technological infrastructures, including campus computer centers and commercial information services." He concludes that "with the reduced importance of physical libraries, librarians and information specialists will need to be proactive and promote special services to user communities.[25] One basic advantage of libraries can be the integration of various sources of information to create one-stop shopping. Information consultant Andrew Garvin, as part of his prescription to what he calls "information paralysis," identifies "four basic types of sources of information: government sources; associations; commercial publishers, services and sources; and libraries and educational institutions."[26] Instead of advising users to consult these sources separately, we need to continue to offer services with resources drawn from all of these sources. Beyond integration, however, libraries have to offer service to users who prefer to work from their offices and homes and not have to take the extra trouble of coming to the library during specified hours. It will become increasingly important that librarians can be reached by their patrons via electronic mail, that librarians can transmit information back to users' computers, and that librarians participate in electronic discussion forums not only those populated by other librarians but also forums focusing on particular subjects.

Even with this growing availability and importance of inter-institutional and international networks, I believe that within each information service core competencies of individuals still will need to be developed and recognized, and this very much includes competencies in the international and foreign area. As Robert Eccles and Richard Nolan have pointed out, the core competencies and expertise infrastructure are "the basis of an organization's competitive advantage," and I believe that this very much includes library organizations.[27] Teamwork will be essential, as the librarian with expertise in international organizations, for example, might need to work with other librarians with expertise in intellectual property, environmental affairs, or any number of fields.

The type of team used is important in dealing with the flow of information. Rather than using the "symphony orchestra" team concept, in which information largely comes from the conductor, the choice needs to be the "doubles tennis team" or "jazz combo" team model, in which the participants receive their information predominantly from each other.[28] At the same time, members of these teams need to be recognized as experts who can be relied upon to develop and utilize technologies, communications with users, and team structures. As Eccles and Nolan further point out, "micromanagement, though rendered possible by this development [modern information technology], is undesirable because it undermines the effective exploitation of the potential value of knowledge workers–that is, stifles innovation and commitment."[29]

Also, we need to consider Michael Schrage's reminder that "however useful and relevant these technologies are to the way an organization manages its information flow . . . there is nothing inherent in these technologies that encourages collaborative relationships."[30] Or, consider the comments of a Microsoft employee who, after asserting that "the future of e-mail usage is being pioneered right here," reveals that "the cool thing with e-mail is that when you send it, there's no possibility of connecting with the person on the other end. It's better than phone answering machines, because with them, the person on the other line might actually pick up the phone and you might have to talk."[31] Electronic mail, whether within an institution or on a world-wide network of experts, retrieval of information from various remote computers, new computer technologies such as "knowbot" software agents, and other valuable technologies are in themselves not sufficient to build the collaborative relationships necessary for teams of experts to succeed.

Recognition of the growing importance of the international and foreign dimension of information services is the first step to addressing adequately these needs. Such recognition should help in building the case for allocating financial resources in this area. Decisions about how much and what type of expertise in international matters is needed in a particular institution need to be made. Core competencies need to be developed and then shared, both within the institution as part of a reference team and on an inter-institutional level by resource sharing and by communication among experts via computer networks. No one person, even an expert in international matters, can be expected to know in-depth a body of information spanning many nations and organizations, languages, and types of formats. However, the very same computer and communications technologies that have in part made the international component of information so indispensable also provide some of the best answers for coping with this avalanche of information. An accurate prediction of how new technologies will change access and analysis of international and foreign information, and information in general, is ultimately a difficult and perhaps impossible task. Danny Hillis, the co-founder and chief scientist of Thinking Machines and a computer visionary, recently noted that " . . . in the early '60s people used to talk about what would happen in the year 2000, and now it's 1993 and people are still talking about what will happen in the year 2000. So the future has been kind of shrinking about one year per year for my whole life! People now realize that 2020 is just going to be so different, that they can't even think about it."[32] Hillis goes on to point out that "We're very much heading toward a two-class society where either you're somebody who sort of knows about, or feels empowered to deal with all of the complexity in society, or you're one of the people that is a victim of it and is just on the receiving end of it all."[33] The problems and approaches discussed in this article certainly fall into this side of millennium barrier, but they are issues deserving of further thought and analysis if librarians want to have a role in helping others understand the complexities of the expanding global community.

NOTES

1. Andrew P. Garvin, *The Art of Being Well-Informed; What You Need to Know to Gain the Winning Edge In Business* (Garden City Park, NY: Avery, 1993), 12.

2. Walter B. Wriston, *The Twilight of Sovereignty; How the Information Revolution is Transforming Our World* (New York: Charles Scribners, 1992), 132, 152.

3. Wendell Berry, *Sex, Economy, Freedom, & Community* (New York: Pantheon Books, 1993), 18.

4. Peter F. Drucker, *Post-Capitalist Society* (New York: Harper Business, 1993), 74.

5. Berry, 37.

6. Daniel McNeill and Paul Freiberger, *Fuzzy Logic* (New York: Simon & Schuster, 1992), 41.

7. Ibid., 44.

8. Richard Saul Wurman, *Information Anxiety; What to Do When Information Doesn't Tell You What You Need to Know* (New York: Bantam Books, 1990), 49.

9. Eugene Skolnikoff, *The Elusive Transformation; Science, Technology, and the Evolution of International Politics* (Princeton: Princeton University Press, 1993), 216.

10. S. Michael Malinconico, "Information's Brave New World," *Library Journal* 117 (May 1, 1992): 40.

11. Thomas H. Reynolds and Arturo A. Flores, *Foreign Law; Current Sources of Codes and Basic Legislation in Jurisdictions of the World* American Association of Law Libraries Publication No. 33. (Littleton, Fred S. Rothman, 1989-1992).

12. *Official Journal of the European Communities* (1989 L 386), 1.

13. Skolnikoff, 94.

14. Ibid., 96-102.

15. Igor Kavass and Adolf Sprudzs, *United States International Treaties Today; Unpublished and Unnumbered Treaties Index 1989* (Buffalo: William S. Hein, 1990), iv.

16. "Reverse Banana Diplomacy; Will the OAS Lead the Charge to D.C. Statehood?" *Washington City Paper* 14 (January 7-14, 1994): 8.

17. Union of International Associations, *Yearbook of International Organizations* (Munich: K.G. Saur, 1948-).

18. *Consolidated Treaties and International Agreements: United States Current Document Service* (Dobbs Ferry, NY: Oceana, 1991-).

Hein's United States Treaties and Other International Agreements Current Service (Buffalo: William S. Hein, 1990-), microfiche.

TIARA CDROM: Treaties and International Agreements Researchers' Archive (Dobbs Ferry, NY: Oceana, 1993-).

USTREATIES database on WESTLAW.

19. *International Legal Materials* (Washington, DC: American Society of International Law, 1962-).

20. Drucker, 56,59.

21. Lewis J. Perelman, *School's Out; Hyperlearning, the New Technology, and the End of Education* (New York, William Morrow, 1992), 59-60.

22. Thomas W. Malone and John F. Rockart, "How Will Information Technology Reshape Organizations? Computers as Coordination Technology," in *Globalization, Technology, and Competition; the Fusion of Computers and Telecommunications in the 1990s,* ed. Stephen P. Bradley, Jerry A. Hausman, and Richard L. Nolan (Boston, Harvard Business School Press, 1993), 51.

23. To join INT-LAW, send the message "subscribe int-law your name" to listserv@vm1.spcs.umn.edu or to listserv@uminn1.bitnet.

24. Sara Robbins and Gregory E. Koster, "The New York Joint International Law Program Experience," *Law Library Journal* 85(4) (Fall 1993): 783-799.

25. Malinconico, 40.

26. Garvin, 112.

27. Robert G. Eccles and Richard L. Nolan, "A Framework for the Design of the Emerging Global Organizational Structure," in *Globalization, Technology, and Competition; the Fusion of Computers and Telecommunications in the 1990s,* ed. Stephen P. Bradley, Jerry A. Hausman, and Richard L. Nolan (Boston: Harvard Business Press, 1993), 63.

28. Drucker, 87-88.

29. Eccles and Nolan, 64.

30. Michael Schrage, *Shared Minds; the Technologies of Collaboration* (New York: Random House, 1990), 146.

31. Douglas Coupland, "Microserfs; Seven Days in the Life of Young Microsoft," *Wired* 2.01 (January 1994): 93.

32. "Kay + Hillis," *Wired* 2.01 (January 1994): 148.

33. Ibid., 149.

The Future of Instruction

Carolyn Dusenbury
Barbara G. Pease

There is much more in the wind than any of us can imagine.

Paul Saffo

What's to become of us? What is our future? There is no shortage of forecasts. Librarianship is awash in speculation about the future of the library, the future of information, the future role and status of librarians, of the reference desk, of library collections. The literature of library instruction contributes its share with articles that discuss the content and efficacy of library instruction, and that attempt to remodel instruction in response to new technologies, and new research on information seekers, learning styles and cognition. Looming over all of this are twin specters: the growing mass of available information and the increasing shortage of money and staff in libraries of all types.

Depictions of the future are diverse, and some are extreme. Instruction librarians are exhorted to master all technologies, to be experts in all known resources, to reach every student–nothing short of single-handedly creating universal information literacy. Then there are those who proclaim the end of librarianship as we know it

Carolyn Dusenbury is Director for Library Services at California State University, Chico, CA. Barbara Pease is Reference Librarian at California State University, Chico, CA.

[Haworth co-indexing entry note]: "The Future of Instruction." Dusenbury, Carolyn, and Barbara G. Pease. Co-published simultaneously in *Journal of Library Administration* (The Haworth Press, Inc.) Vol. 20, Nos. 3/4, 1995, pp. 97-117; and: *The Future of Information Services* (ed: Virginia Steel, and C. Brigid Welch) The Haworth Press, Inc., 1995, pp. 97-117. Multiple copies of this article/chapter may be purchased from The Haworth Document Delivery Center [1-800-3-HAWORTH; 9:00 a.m. - 5:00 p.m. (EST)].

because we cannot possibly compete with the information marketplace. Vague and sinister "others" will usurp our place. There are
also those who leave it all to information technology to provide the
ideal, universal, perfect system to make the need for instruction
obsolete. The first is too exhausting, the second too depressing, and
the third too fatalistic to provide a constructive way to envision the
future.

In this article we will briefly describe the three fundamental
forces that affect instruction: the learner or information seeker,
technology, and the library and librarian. We will also offer some
questions and ideas about what effect these forces may have on
library instruction, and suggest some visions and applications for
the future. We will be looking approximately ten years ahead. It is
important to remember that the future is a continuum. Five years
down the road looks very different from fifty years. Too often,
discussions of the future founder (or discussants come close to
exchanging blows) when one person sees only the short-term and
the other only the long-term future. The issue of what instruction
should be called will not be discussed here. The current debate
about the limitations of the terms "library instruction" or "bibliographic instruction" are important, but resolution of this issue is
happily left to others. It should also be disclaimed that this is written
by academic librarians. While it is hoped that others will find something useful, the academic point-of-view is predominant.

Basically, a model of library instruction is the relationships
among three factors. First, there is the information seeker and
information-seeking behavior. Second, there is information in all its
manifestations: recorded knowledge down through the ages and
data as fresh as last week's statistics; books, microfilm, video,
audio, charts, maps, photographs, and, increasingly, electronic text
and images. Every one of these formats, except the book, requires
special equipment to use. Increasingly the equipment needed is a
computer. Third is the librarian and the library. The library is a
physical place where information is collected, organized, and made
available for use. And it is increasingly a virtual space, a point of
access, one of many perhaps, for information stored within its walls
and elsewhere. Beyond physical and virtual space, the library is an

organization of human beings who put needed information, or the skills for finding and using it, into the hands of library users.

The interaction among these parts has been pretty straightforward, but over the past few years there has been a pervasive mood of change. The call for educational reform, the rapid advances in information technology, the recognition of the diversity of learners, and static or declining resources have created a different environment in all respects. A personal computer has been added to the considerable and essential impedimenta of many students. Students are increasingly involved in distance education programs. How do we instruct students that we do not see in our libraries? Networked information and the emergence of full-text electronic sources enable learners to communicate in new ways and to access new resources. The library is not just a destination, it is also a doorway to this world of information. There are more non-traditional learners and more who speak different languages and share different cultural traditions. As in all parts of education, instruction is similarly more contextual than ever.

The implications for instruction are profound. Because the pace of change is so breathtaking, everything we do today is transitory. We are not finding solutions for all time, but adapting to new developments as they unfold. Students are in the same situation. They are as anxious as we are about what to do to be truly prepared for a constantly changing future. Information literacy will not be a unitary condition that one either possesses or does not; it will be a continuing process of learning, and instruction will be called upon to prepare students not only for the time they are in the education system but for a lifetime in the information age.

THE INFORMATION SEEKER
AND NEW MODELS OF EDUCATING

Since the future of instruction is closely joined, in some ways dependent upon, the expectations of today's and tomorrow's information seekers, what exactly do we know, or can we surmise about this group? They will be an increasingly diverse and multicultural group. Some will be highly computer literate, articulate and demanding of services. Others will be computer naive, but know what they want. Still others may not know that what they need even exists. College students will be older, perhaps returning to school for additional training. As adult learners they will have different motivations than younger or first-time learners. More and more of them will be aware of and ready to use (or learn to use) technology.

We have already seen that most students do not fear technology, but instead ascribe almost magical powers to it. If something is not found in a paper source it might be found elsewhere. If something is not found in an electronic source it does not exist. The computer is synonymous with the information it accesses and is unimpeachable. A high percentage of learners will steadfastly resist any attempt to persuade them to use a printed source even when no exact computer equivalent exists. Today's students want answers and are impatient with complex retrieval of information. Tomorrow's students will be more so. Today's learners have experienced new entertainment media that use multimedia and electronics to provide stunning visual effects and a rapid pace. Will they not expect as much in their information environment? Another aspect of tomorrow's learners may be their willingness to collaborate. We have all seen students huddled around a CD-ROM workstation, collaboratively selecting the references for their group presentation. There is a level of excitement as they interact among themselves and with the terminal. Students also willingly coach each other in the use of CD-ROMs. The computer is a flexible medium–it can encourage collaboration as easily as it can encourage isolation. Should not instruction librarians be exploiting this aspect of the medium?

New educational models are emerging in response to the new reality of information use. Traditional models of education viewed students as, more or less, empty heads into which teachers poured knowledge. This knowledge was cumulative, linear, and prescribed. Desirable behaviors and outcomes were planned, and the education was transmitted from the teacher to the learner. The new cognitive models of education recognize that every student brings a unique set of motivations, expectations and desired outcomes to the educational process. In short, the students are participants in the process rather than passive recipients of recorded knowledge.[1] These new educational models feature critical thinking and collaborative learning where students are taught how to think about information and knowledge by a process of evaluation and synthesis. This is not a linear process, but a constantly adjusted, interactive framework where ideas are re-examined and re-formed with experience and information. Librarians experience this model in practice whenever they monitor students using CD-ROM's. A student types in a word and in seconds may have found 100 items or none. The quick feedback allows them to apply critical thinking–to try other word combinations, read the screen, or ask for assistance–in an attempt to get their search back on track. If we leave them alone, they will eventually retrieve something they can use. Or, if we intervene at that teachable moment before frustration has taken over, but when they realize their search is not as successful as it might be, we may make an impact. We may become collaborators with them, and we may even teach the user something that can be used again in a different situation.

One of the difficulties with collaboration as an instructional mode is that true collaboration requires the parties to be equally prepared to participate. To apply collaboration in a library instruction setting, the librarian must relinquish some control to the learner. Perhaps what will be learned at the teachable moment will not be what the librarian intends; perhaps the pace of the lesson will have to be adapted to the learner's ability or stress level. And learners must assume more responsibility for their own learning by committing the time necessary to learn, or by coming to the encounter prepared to learn.

The teachable moment: it is the optimal time when a learner is ready to learn and is the best, perhaps the only, opportunity to teach. Capitalizing on the teachable moment is not as abstract as it seems. In instruction, it is the time when the information seeker cannot meet an information need and is ready for instruction to make the connection. This is problematic for traditional forms of instruction, which are designed to teach the student now to answer the unanticipated question in the future. Librarians encounter endless teachable moments at a reference desk, and in the process of answering the articulated question also hope to impart the generalizability of this situation to future questions. Some have suggested that recognition of the importance of the teachable moment renders traditional forms of instruction useless exercises, and costly ones, too.

The teachable moment is a realization of need combined with the learner's motivation to meet the need. In 1977, Patrick Wilson described the motivation of learners in *Public Knowledge and Private Ignorance*.[2] While much has been said in the interim, Wilson's framework is as true now and in the future as it was then. Each person has a desire to avoid "costly ignorance." When we think we have enough information, act on the basis of that information, and suffer costly consequences as a result of it, we are victims of costly ignorance. The effort we are willing to expend depends on the consequences. Ignorance that is harmless is of no concern.

In meeting an information need each person has three informational support systems to call upon. The "monitor system" uses personal observation and communication in conjunction with the sources one uses routinely (e.g., magazines, television) to gain information at the desired level. It is both purposeful and incidental. The "reserve system" consists of sources that may never be used but which are available if the need arises. For most learners, the library is a reserve system. The third is the "advisory system," made up of those who are able to advise regarding a specific decision. Advisors provide counsel in addition to information. Physicians, librarians, teachers, and accountants function in an advisory system. The key player is the learner, who uses each of the systems in different ways and for different needs. However, one thing is manifest–the learner does not seek the ultimately advantageous outcome, but will usually choose the easiest acceptable solution. The motivation to mitigate costly ignorance is dependent on the importance of the outcome. If the decision is critical to the learner's well-being, the learner exerts greater effort toward the most advantageous outcome. Wilson further postulates something that is painful for librarians. "The need for a search for new sources . . . is a sign of failure of one's information system . . . Far from welcoming occasions for search, one wants no such occasions at all."[3] It can be postulated that there is a hierarchy of desirability of these systems. The most preferred is the monitor system where one's existing knowledge is sufficient to meet the need. The next most preferred is the advisory system. You can go to someone for advice as well as information and save yourself the tedious task of gathering and synthesizing information. The reserve system requires the most effort. The idea of ignorance as a measure of effort is important. Costly ignorance is ignorance in the usual sense of not knowing that something exists at all and of thinking that something means something that it does not. It is also ignorance in a slightly different sense, the knowledge that "it" is out there somewhere but we can't get there, and it is just too much trouble to find out how.

Students trust computers. They have confidence in technology. Computers (in their view) give them answers quickly, or just as quickly point out when a search has failed and a new search must be formulated. When students assess the results of their information searches, they also assess their level of costly ignorance. They make judgments as active participants in the information gathering process; whether to spend more time, seek more or different information, or use what they have. The decisions are theirs. Thus, an important role for instruction is the concept of making decisions and the consequences of them. Students soon learn the consequences of an unstructured search in a large database. They will either be satisfied with the first few citations that come close enough or they will attempt to refine the search to more exactly match their question. The power of technology is that students expect good results and have faith that the answer is in there somewhere. So rather than walk away unsatisfied, we already have students ask more than "what computer do I use to find some articles on . . . " They are moving to "which database do you recommend for articles about . . . " or "where ELSE could I look for . . . " In this way, the technology is forcing many users to change their view of information access. Our instructional efforts will inevitably change with them.

TECHNOLOGY AND RESOURCES

There is costly ignorance when using computers too. To assume that everything you may need will be in one database, or will be available using a computerized index is just one form of this ignorance. Ignorance about the rules and conventions of any computerized system can lead to a false impression of what is available, as well as wasted time in retrieving it. Given the incredible amount of information that exists now, and the rapidity with which more is generated, it is clear that taming the beast will not be easy.

> To give some sense of the scale, the collections of the Library of Congress contain nearly 100 million items . . . that's something like 100 terabits of information. Let's call that amount of information 1 "Library of Congress," abbreviated as "LC." It has taken over two centuries to amass that one LC. . . . NASA's information store is currently growing at the rate of 63 terabits annually. . . . The medical imaging machines of the United States produce 1 LC every week or so.[4]

Futurists point to technology as the tool to control this deluge, but instruction librarians are not sanguine. Donald Langenberg, writing about the impact of technology on scholars and researchers says "[L]earning to use information technology requires a large investment in time and effort before the investment pays off, and help is hard to find."[5] Technology itself is complicated and using a complicated system to access a complicated system of many, many information resources appears to be a morass to many users.

The great promise of technology is that it will significantly simplify or eliminate some of the more complicated or repetitive skills students now have to learn and librarians have to teach; Z39.50 and future developments in this area are well within the 10-year time frame and hold the promise of a single user interface for all systems. The downside is that, at first, there may be several common interfaces competing for acceptance. If you have an ABC system in your library, for example, your learners will do fine until they need information at a non-ABC site. How many levels out from home base can or should instruction librarians incorporate in their teaching? Looking beyond 10 years, however, it is possible that one system will become so attractive that it will become a universal standard notwithstanding proprietary interests.

The arrival of full text will end some of the run-around that is boring to teach and to learn. When the learner can hit the display key and get the full text of an article from a citation, instruction librarians will no longer have to explain that (1) now you must find out if the library subscribes to the periodical, (2) periodicals may be in three places–current, bound, or microformat–unless (3) they are off the shelf or at the bindery or the article has been "liberated," in which case you might want to (4) go to Interlibrary Loan or find another library not far away that has the title.

Duplication of resources on various systems, however, is likely to remain a problem for some time to come given the rapid and unrestrained growth of networked resources. An Internet excursion through Gopherspace will yield multiple *ERICs* and even more *CIA Factbooks*. But how many *ERIC's* do you need? A reasonable question and a profound one similar to the debates about the virtue of having 500 cable television channels, 30 of which are, at the same time, showing the same episode of *Gilligan's Island*. One response to the question might be that multiple versions of one database allow users to choose the interface with which they are most comfortable, or which provides the quickest way to the kind of information they seek. For example, comparing the SilverPlatter version of *ERIC* to the CARL version we find that CARL offers searching by target audience which SilverPlatter does not. We may also find that some people prefer the CARL interface while others prefer Silver-Platter's, while others prefer the source with the lowest telephone charges. Another response might be that duplication of resources simply means more "noise" that someone must filter out. It leads us to ask if we are truly navigating the Internet, moving purposefully from location to location, or if we are surfing, riding with the waves without any real destination, or hanging on to our life rafts, trying desperately not to go under. How will this phantasmagoria of information and data be organized so that a learner can find the best information for a purpose?

Patrick Wilson also had something important to say about finding the best information.[6] The learner's power over information and data can be called bibliographical control. While the term bibliographic is now suspect because of its traditional suggestion of physical rather than virtual objects, Wilson's point is that the learner controls the information rather than the other way around. Two possibilities exist. The first is the ability to identify all existing writings fitting a certain description–called "descriptive control" by Wilson. The second is the ability to find the best information to an end–"exploitative control." These are not equal states:

I suggest that, apart from the desire to be able to indulge one's whims and idle curiosity, the only reason for desiring [descriptive] power is as a substitute for the other, greater, but less easily obtainable power. The only reason for wanting to line up a population in arbitrary ways is that one lacks the other power, and has oneself to attempt discovery of the best . . . means to one's ends by scrutiny of members of various neutrally described classes of the population.[7]

What Wilson suggests is that being able, in some sense, to subdue and describe a massive amount of information–to be able to present the learner with 500 or 5000 different items matching a description is a vastly inferior outcome than being able to present the learner with the 12 or 15 sources that come the closest to meeting the information need. To present a learner with the entire networked universe is an interesting technical exercise and a powerful demonstration of the scope of technology, but it doesn't really begin to do the job of finding the best text. Karen Takle Quinn, speaking at the annual symposium for Graduate Alumni and Faculty of the Rutgers School of Communication, Information, and Library Studies, made the point that "just making the information available is not enough, but making the information more useful is key."[8]

Computer technology with its present speed and matching capabilities, makes descriptive control, even of thousands upon thousands of items, easy. It can line up more objects matching a description than can be read in a lifetime. But what can it do to line up all those things in order of relevance to a specific request? James D. Anderson suggests a future direction for information technology away from Boolean logic and toward natural language and weighted searching, in which computers respond to queries with a ranked response based on the characteristics of the source or the number of uses of a term. Although known for some time, very few of the common information retrieval systems use these methods.[9]

Either information technology will discover a way to establish the criterion of relevance for information retrieval or information seekers, themselves, will tend to limit themselves to the tools that they are familiar with. In the meantime, the critical job of evaluating sources will perhaps be made more manageable when libraries and librarians, having created their own networks, and having tied them to campus-wide information systems, and wide-area information systems, begin to pass on to their users some of the knowledge that will be learned about how to make choices and distinguish among various seemingly similar resources. This new knowledge will then form part of the new curriculum of critical thinking and information literacy. Developments in these areas are critical to the success of the information revolution. Until then . . . consider the words of that renowned philosopher, Mike Royko:

> I have just returned from a journey that left my eyes bugging, my head spinning and me being hopelessly lost . . . bumbling around an eerie place you may have read or heard about. It is Internet . . . all you need, the pitch goes, is a computer, a modem and a telephone line . . .
>
> There is more information on the electronic superhighway than you could absorb in 1,000 years of reading . . . and all of this fascinating knowledge will come leaping out of your computer screen, into your eyes, onto your brain and make you smart as the dickens . . .
>
> I've been forced to learn the basics of computing . . . but only recently did I rev up and peel rubber onto Internet . . . As far as I can tell, I didn't get halfway up the first entrance ramp. After getting a cordial welcome on my screen, I was given the "Sig menu." I didn't know who or what Sig was. The last Sig I knew played right field on my softball team and could drink beer like an elephant sucking water.
>
> The Sig menu gave me another menu of places . . . I picked one and got another menu. Then another and another. I still wasn't anywhere.
>
> I finally arrived somewhere and this is what I got: "in the archie system version 3 of the telnet and email client access a common set of commands. Additionally, there are specialized commands specific to the particular interfaces. See the Interactive Interface and the Email interface sections below for a list of these commands . . . "
>
> Forget it. I have never been to "telnet stis.nsf.gov," and I don't plan on going.[10]

"It's all very complicated." These are the words of Theodor
Nelson who has been one of the leading visionaries and futurists in
computer system design. "It's all very complicated" is part and
parcel of the "technoid vision," which is:

- We'll have wonderful, wonderful things; and
- They'll get more and more complicated.
- I get credit for this complication, he gets credit for that complication, and we don't even know who created the other complications; and
- You have to learn it the way we're going to stuff it to you,
  because that is the destiny of technology.[11]

Further, "The same myth spawns 'sophistication.' Technoids use
sophistication to mean some curious combination of powerful and
complicated . . . anything good must be complicated."[12]

Nelson says emphatically that it doesn't have to be this way.
There is a curious culture of complication in the design of computer
systems that is unnecessary. When these items are not called computers, they aren't so complicated. For instance, "we call them CD
players so we will not have to know that they are computers . . . We
are increasingly the prisoners of the clever wonks who are able to
memorize all the bizarre tangles, complications and exceptions to
the pieces of software disguised as real objects. The technoids carry
with them the keys . . . "[13] And the worst sin of all for Nelson, is
that the wonks are rewarded for creating it.

Will this do as a given state of affairs for most learners? It will
not, but the emphasis remains adding more and more things to a
hopelessly complicated infrastructure. Everyone seems to agree that
a tool enabling a user to navigate the Internet rather than just muck-
ing around will be a breakthrough in the use of electronic information. Until then, consumers will certainly vote with their feet using
the costly ignorance principle. Whatever I can get using a system I
can understand is infinitely preferable to having better sources in a
system that is impenetrable.

Is the typical library, as James Rettig has stated, "a prima facie
manifestation of the technoid paradigm?"[14] Have librarians been
too complacent in accepting design complications and trying to
mitigate them by constructing elaborate end-user training devices

and programs? Do we design those pages and pages (or their equivalent) that sit next to workstations because we really believe that most of our users will read them? Perhaps they assuage our frustration that we feel helpless in the face of this complexity.

THE LIBRARY AND THE LIBRARIAN

How will the library, the third element of the triad, impact library instruction. Will it change or disappear? Will librarians' work change significantly in the face of new options for information access and delivery?

Libraries at present provide a structure for a certain kind of information, print or "near print," i.e., microform. This kind of information can be in only one place at a time, and people must come to it in order to use it. The larger and more diverse the collection of information objects, the more complicated the organizational scheme of the library, and the more important the librarians' role. Librarians help people find the objects they need, whether through accurate cataloging, a reference interview, or instruction in the kinds of materials and services that the library provides and how to use them. Librarians design and maintain this information environment in order to be useful to people. They teach users to understand and conform to the environment's rules in order for the users to be independent within it.

With the advent of the computer and electronic information, the single information object can be accessed in many different ways and displayed in many places at once. The information comes to the seeker, and information seekers need not all follow the same path to the information. They need not come to the library at all. Information seekers suddenly have a high degree of independence from the librarians' carefully prepared and maintained environment. Information itself will be (and is already) less linear, less bound by hierarchy.

Will librarians embrace this independence as they design instruction programs or will they resist? Can we continue to expect users to conform to a single model of research, the start-general-and-narrow-as-you-go model? Can we continue to expect users to come to our place at our pre-set time in order to learn what they need to learn? Can we expect all users to be equally motivated or equally ready to learn at the same time? These questions combined with staff and budget shortages are causing careful re-examination of how resources are deployed and how effective current programs are.

Some suggest that libraries are threatened by the emerging private information services such as Prodigy and America Online. Is this really a new development? There have always been alternative information systems. The development of widely available, efficient, and economical alternatives may have been oversold as a change in the information landscape. In the same way that it is easier to read a magazine if you have a personal subscription, these systems are tailored to a mass audience, they are easy to use, and they are convenient–they are always open and information is easily retrieved. It seems likely that such systems will meet the needs of those users who are willing to pay for these features. To consumers, these services fit their definition of libraries, and they will think of them as libraries.

It is clear that libraries and the work of librarians must evolve in order to remain relevant in the age of information. However, there is a long tradition in libraries, of complicating things, of hiding the prize and then showing users the path they should take to that prize. In part this is because organizing a collection of diverse materials is a complex task, yet this should not blind librarians to the possibility of simplifying things when the possibility exists. Remember those first laser-disc *Infotrac* systems? Students lined up to use them because they were easy to use, almost fun, and you didn't have to hand write your citations. Many librarians, however, lamented that the indexing was poor, and that students mistakenly thought that *Infotrac* was the answer to every assignment or research paper. *Infotrac* is no longer the only computerized database. Students are able to see that other equally convenient and possibly better tools exist. Now if it is the most used database, it is probably safe to say that it is, after all, a reasonable and efficacious tool for the task. Today, you can subscribe to an index with several hundred titles available in full text; you can distribute this index around your campus or community. If the interface is even fairly friendly, most users will be able to retrieve citations and text with no outside instruction at all. Will librarians say, "Good, now there is a simple system for those who aren't willing to learn complicated search and retrieval." Or will they say, "If we give this to our users, they will love it, but they will mistakenly think that these 400 periodicals are all there are, and they won't use anything else. They won't always be using the best sources of information." The first response makes things simple, it is user centered. The second makes things complicated, library centered. Similarly, some librarians "despair over the very broad free-text searches users content themselves with instead of doing carefully crafted Boolean searches. . . . In other words, they don't think these users have found . . . 'the correct answer'."[15]

If some of our users can figure out, on their own, how to access the information they want—perhaps not perfectly but enough to meet their needs, by their own definition—should librarians deny these users this option or give up instruction entirely? Perhaps, instead, we should take as an instructional goal making users aware of their choices and of the differences among those choices. The issue is not that users will apply the costly ignorance principle, it is whether they know enough about their information options to make an informed choice. Perhaps the most important thing instruction can do is make the user aware that they have choices, that they in fact, choose all the time, whether by omission or by commission.

For librarians to evolve and stay ahead of the curve of change, they must begin to try on new roles. One role that has been suggested is to involve themselves in system design and to participate in the development of products on the front end, rather than coping with the finished product. Librarians have rarely if ever, been present at the creation of products. Libraries are not such significant players in the market that their opinions significantly affect publishing decisions. In spite of the few library publishers who sometimes solicit our counsel, libraries are not a primary market for new electronic information systems. The producers want to go where the money is—the mass market of end-users. It is difficult to imagine how librarians will significantly ingratiate themselves into the design process of commercial products, despite the exhortations to do so. Libraries could conceivable play this role, however, especially if grouped into significantly large consortia to impact a commercial producer's revenues. Libraries and librarians might also begin to approach the design end, not with commercial products, but with library or campus wide products, such as catalog front ends, CWIS, WAIS, and Gopher and Internet products such as Veronica and the subject trees currently being talked about. Individual librarians might begin to experiment with hypermedia and CAI which can be integrated into a traditional user education program, like the Biology CAI programs developed at the University of California, Riverside.[16]

One of the problems with envisioning new ways of doing things is that frequently our libraries lack the facilities necessary to implement the new ways. Although libraries have computers, are they networked campus or city-wide? Do we have, have we even conceived of, hypermedia lecture halls and interactive hypermedia laboratories and design centers for producing and disseminating new instructional media?[17] Do librarians themselves have the skills to utilize such facilities?

Changes in library instruction can't be made alone. They must be part of an overall organizational vision or plan. Such a plan establishes priorities, allocates resources, and can provide the structure in which staff can develop the expertise necessary to attempt new ways of doing things. Because libraries have become less departmentalized as they have lost personnel, there is often a freer interchange among work groups. Interdepartmental task groups are more common, and can be a medium for experimenting with new roles.

Even if librarians do relinquish some complexity in favor of greater ease for the end-user; even if they do relinquish control and become more collaborative with the information seeker; even if they confront, and perhaps radically change their ideas about what should be taught in the new information environment, there is still one other important issue they must confront in the next ten years: the issue of outcomes assessment and performance measures. Librarians will be under greater and greater pressure to prove that instruction works. Our affective feelings and the positive feedback of users will not suffice. Instruction librarians are true believers in what they do, and true believers are not the best judges of the fruit of their labors. Success in the information age will require more than the mastery of skills. It will require an ability to gather, evaluate, and synthesize information into knowledge. The easiest thing to measure, however, is the mastery of skills. Will librarians fall back on the easily measurable, because of the potentially dangerous consequences for the library's resource base if we try and fail to measure true learning? Just how do we measure the ability of learners to be effective information synthesizers? This is one of the most important issues on the horizon for instruction librarians.

CONCLUSION

What is in the future for library instruction? How can librarians work toward shaping its and their futures? By taking a snapshot of a typical instruction session today, we can begin to see how it will change. This session consists of a number of parts. In addition to the introduction to the library and the librarian as a resource person, the librarian will probably:

1. Introduce the conceptual framework of information and the nature of the literature of the discipline.
2. Describe various types of resources (catalog, index, reference works), their purposes and why they would be used.
3. Demonstrate the catalog and an index–probably electronic versions of both.
4. Explain how to retrieve information using the call number or the citation.
5. Talk about search strategy for the class assignment if there is one.
6. Mention diverse other topics such as special collections, how to make photocopies, where to get change, an orientation to where things are in the building, and so on.

Any instruction librarian will tell you that this is already a full agenda. Add downloading, Internet, and Gophers and the task approaches impossible. Usually, this is our only shot at instruction, so we have to make the most of it. But is it any wonder that we see a lot of these same students a few days later at the reference desk asking for a repeat of part of the presentation?

Technology will, in fact, make part of this presentation unnecessary. If the catalog and other resources use a common interface, only one system will have to be taught. The availability of full-text resources will not require elaborate retrieval explanations. In many incremental ways, much of the information we transmit will be simplified. Helpful certainly, but not the stuff of our electronic dreams.

The real power of technology is the integration of instruction, sources, media, and computing. Imagine a novice student sitting down at a workstation and clicking on a "hello" icon. This takes him to a video of a librarian who explains the preliminaries and how the integrated system works. The next step is a menu of choices: a video tour of the library, an explanation/demonstration of the campus information network, and choices for beginning a search for information. This last choice leads the student through a multimedia presentation on any aspect of the traditional instruction session and is interactive. When the student runs into an unfamiliar concept there is a dictionary, encyclopedia, or other reference tool available with a click. There are multimedia tutorials for the resources. When the student finds a book that sounds really good or the journal article that sounds perfect, the system will lead him to related materials, some of which will be full-text, but there will also be still images, video clips, and graphics. There are similar information systems for using software such as database management programs, graphics programs, and so forth. Of course, the completed project is sent to the teacher electronically for evaluation. We hasten to add that the student can move around completely independently. There is a path to follow but the system is entirely flexible in where the student enters, maneuvers, and exits.

This sounds like education that is never touched by human hands . . . but it is possible within the ten-year horizon we have set: is there anything wrong with this picture?

If this is the only alternative, it is not a happy future for students or for librarians who tend to be fairly sociable. Not every student wants to, has the ability to, or has the equipment to sit in isolation communicating with cyberspace. Even the most sophisticated system will not be completely self-contained. Many users will still need a person to communicate with when they need assistance and a place to go to be around other people if he or she gets tired of his or her own company.

However, the system described does meet a number of important conditions. It is interactive and allows the student to be independent or collaborative. Instruction is introduced at the moment it is needed and because it is part of a real world assignment there is immediate reinforcement. The system is not complicated, it can meet the standard of exploitative control by providing information that is not merely similar but related. It also satisfies many of the issues raised by the costly ignorance principle. This is the resource that a majority of students will happily use as their monitor system.

Will there still be a reserve system, a building with printed stuff in it called the library? Almost certainly yes. It will also have people in it and provide the workstations for those who do not have them. But just as Wilson suggested, it will be the reserve system . . . just as it is now.

Having established that this new system, let's call it Omni, is possible within ten years, is it likely? This is the real question. Libraries cannot shut down all of their current enterprises and begin a national initiative to develop Omni. We still have a job to do. Individual libraries will not have the resources to design an entire version of Omni at each place, even large consortia would be pressed to get it done. The market may decide that there is enough reward in creating Omni. If one company were to succeed it is almost frightening to think of how much power it would have.

Omni will probably be the work of many hands. Someone, somewhere, will develop a piece of software and put it on the network for others. Someone else will tinker with it, and then someone else. When one thinks of the development of Archie, Veronica, or Gopher one can be almost optimistic that if not Omni, at least Sort-of-Omni, will be born in our working lives. The good news is that there are creative people, visionaries, futurists and designers working on precisely this problem. It also helps that most of the pieces exist already. The text resources, the video, the instruction modules all exist in some format and can be digitized. Omni is not entirely a job of creation–it is a job of synthesis and integration. Librarians will play a role since they are the most experienced information instructors, but the true designers of the system will be the masses of users. The systems that work best for them will be the ones that succeed. If the information highway is to become a reality, Omni is what we will all be driving.

And for all those skeptics who remind us that it was once said that when we all had safe, unlimited nuclear power, electricity would be too cheap to meter, remind them of the oft-told tale that if automobile technology and costs had developed and changed like computer technology, a Mercedes would get 500 miles to the gallon and cost 300 dollars.

NOTES

1. For a discussion of learning theory and a bibliography of other sources on this topic see, Arp, Lori, "An Introduction to Learning Theory," in *Sourcebook for Bibliographic Instruction,* ed. Katherine Branch (Chicago: Association of College and Research Libraries, 1993), p. 5-14.

2. Wilson, Patrick. *Public Knowledge and Private Ignorance: Toward a Library and Information Policy* (Westport, CT: Greenwood Press, 1977).

3. Ibid., p. 84.

4. Langenberg, Donald N., "The Lonely Scholar in a Global Information Environment," in *New Technologies and New Directions: Proceedings from the Symposium on Scholarly Communication, The University of Iowa, November 14-16, 1991,* ed. G.R. Boynton and Sheila D. Creth (Westport. CT: Meckler, 1993), p. 29.

5. Ibid., p. 33.

6. Wilson, Patrick. *Two Kinds of Power: An Essay on Bibliographic Control* (Berkeley, CA: University of California Press, 1968).

7. Ibid., pp. 25-26.

8. Quinn, Karen Takle. "Information Literacy in the Workplace: Education/ Training Considerations," in *Information Literacy: Learning How to Learn: Proceedings of the twenty eighth annual symposium of the Graduate Alumni and Faculty of the Rutgers School of Communication, Information and Library Studies, April 6, 1990.* ed. Jana Varlejs (Jefferson, NC, McFarland & Co, 1991), p. 19.

9. "Discussion: Panel and Audience" in *Information Literacy: Learning How to Learn: Proceedings of the twenty eighth annual symposium of the Graduate Alumni and Faculty of the Rutgers School of Communication, Information and Library Studies, April 6, 1990.* ed. Jana Varlejs (Jefferson, NC: McFarland & Co., 1991), p. 58.

10. Royko, Mike, "Out of Control on the Information Highway," *Sacramento Bee* (24 November 1993), Scene, p. 2.

11. Nelson, Theodor, "Freedom and Power," in *New Technologies and New Directions: Proceedings from the Symposium on Scholarly Communication, The University of Iowa, November 14-16, 1991,* ed. G.R. Boynton and Sheila D. Creth (Westport, CT: Meckler, 1993), p. 2.

12. Ibid., p. 3.

13. Ibid.

14. Rettig, James, "To BI or not to BI–That is the Question," in *Rethinking Reference in Academic Libraries: Proceedings and Process of Library Solutions Institute No. 2, University of California, March 12-14, 1993,* ed. Anne Lipow (Berkeley, CA: Library Solutions Press, 1993), p. 143.

15. Ibid, p. 144.

16. Cooper, John A. "Using CAI to Teach Library Skills, *C&RL News*, 54:2, February 1993, pp. 75-78.

17. Kolitsky, Michael A, "Integration of Hypermedia Across the Curriculum," in *New Technologies and New Directions: Proceedings of the Symposium on Scholarly Communication, University of Iowa, Nov. 14-16, 1991,* ed. G.R. Boynton and Sheila D. Creth (Westport, CT: Meckler Corp., 1993), p. 80.

Library and Information Studies Education for the 21st Century Practitioner

Jeffrey T. Huber

INTRODUCTION

Restructuring educational orientation in schools of library and information studies to reflect technological advances and the changing nature of the profession is a topic of growing concern. In general, however, there is little agreement among educators and practitioners as to what a new curriculum should include. Educators tend to believe that master's degree programs–whether it be those that are more traditional in nature or those that have actively embraced emerging information technologies–should expose students to the theoretical framework that supports the discipline. Practitioners generally are in favor of competency-based studies that prepare students to apply what they have learned during their academic endeavors using tools commonly found in the work environment. These two views regarding the objectives of a master's degree program in library and information studies are not mutually exclusive. Unfortunately, the continued growth and development of information technologies have made it more and more difficult to incorporate a global view of practical application given the time constraints under which most MLIS programs operate. In addition,

Jeffrey T. Huber is Assistant Professor, School of Library and Information Studies, Texas Woman's University, Denton, TX.

[Haworth co-indexing entry note]: "Library and Information Studies Education for the 21st Century Practitioner." Huber, Jeffrey T. Co-published simultaneously in *Journal of Library Administration* (The Haworth Press, Inc.) Vol. 20, Nos. 3/4, 1995, pp. 119-130; and: *The Future of Information Services* (ed: Virginia Steel, and C. Brigid Welch) The Haworth Press, Inc., 1995, pp. 119-130. Multiple copies of this article/chapter may be purchased from The Haworth Document Delivery Center [1-800-3-HAWORTH; 9:00 a.m. - 5:00 p.m. (EST)].

the nature of the profession is changing so as to envelope a multidisciplinary and interdisciplinary approach to the provision of information services. The future of information creation, organization, storage, retrieval, and dissemination will directly affect the content and structure of education for information services providers preparing for work in the 21st century; but the exact nature of that curriculum remains in question. There are several factors, though, that provide insight as to possible directions education in this field may take as it is impacted by advancing technologies, and as a cross-discipline approach strengthens for the provision of information services. Ultimately, though, it is inevitable that the field of study offered by each school or college of library and information studies will evolve to mirror the emerging needs of future practitioners.

BACKGROUND

Curriculum

Curriculum represents the collective body of courses offered by a school or college to qualify students for admission to the field. It typically consists of a number of required classes thought necessary to provide a foundation in library and information studies–known as the core curriculum–accompanied by various elective courses that allow students to specialize in a particular area that falls within the scope of the profession. The area of specialization may be based on type of library or information center, function of position within the library or information center, or a combination of the two. While the stable of courses may vary among schools, the general function of the curriculum remains constant–to educate its students. "It [the curriculum] embodies its [the school's] definition of the professions' knowledge base and asserts its values" (Stieg 1992, 106). The curriculum functions within the school to instruct its students, while the school operates within the broader context of the profession to produce future practitioners. This kinship has not changed dramatically since the inception of library and information studies as a profession. What has evolved is the content of the curriculum based largely upon advancing technologies. The curriculum employed in the education of future information services providers reflects the

mission, goals, and objectives of each individual school as circum-
scribed by practice. The profession, to a great extent, defines the
field of study with the school administering the actual curriculum.
Curriculum, school, profession–one does not exist devoid of the
others. There is a distinct relationship that binds the three; and this
connection is significant given the challenges and opportunities
facing the profession. "In that light, library and information science
education must very simply always be in a proactive position of
identifying needed change and then act as a change agent by providing the intellectual environment and stimulus for the analysis of that
change and the applications which will occur" (Stueart 1989, 391).

Restructuring the Curriculum for the Future

The curriculum for MLIS programs must be restructured to reflect
evolving information infrastructures and the complexities of information delivery confronting future services providers. "The core
of library and information science education remains the single
binding force to the concept of service access to information"
(Stueart 1989, 392). However, this "core" must reflect current
trends in the profession. The field, as well as society at large, has
rapidly become one that is tied closely to computing and technology. Technology has altered the way man thinks, organizes knowledge, and disseminates information. Automation has affected virtually all aspects of the profession, and the technology driving
automation is currently constantly advancing whether through computing enhancements or application innovations.

It is necessary to understand the theories and concepts underlying
emerging technologies in order to grasp practical application given
the continuous flux in computing and automation. This is not to say,
however, that the education process should–or possibly could–include formal instruction in every information technology application. Rather, the objective must be to teach basic concepts within
the context of the theoretical underpinnings of the profession and
how to apply those concepts in a practical setting. Instead of graduating students who meet a set stock of competencies–many of
which become outdated rapidly–educators must teach students to
ask questions, think about problems, analyze situations, and apply
the knowledge they possess. Given this, it would be beneficial to

examine educational models and philosophies adopted or revisited by other disciplines that have already begun to address the problems associated with abundant information and advancing technologies as they consider preparing practitioners for the 21st century.

EDUCATIONAL MODELS AND PHILOSOPHIES

Problem-Based Learning

One educational model that has proven successful in graduating students who can adapt and function in a rapidly changing environment is problem-based learning (PBL). PBL is based on research concerning the most effective methods of adult education, and has been adopted by a variety of disciplines including many of those in the health sciences. It has fallen under the guise of various headings other than PBL such as self-directed learning, self-managed learning, student-centered learning, contract learning, and experiential learning. No matter the term, the objective is the same—to develop links between theory and practice in a meaningful way (Creedy 1992, 727).

In using problem-based learning as an educational model, an environment is created in which theory and practice are not taught as separate activities but as complementary factors with each supporting the other. Teaching methodologies are employed that demonstrate the relationship between the two and promote self-directed learning, reasoning, and conceptual comprehension. It is a form of education in which students learn information in the same context in which it is to be applied. Contextual learning has been shown to facilitate acquiring, retaining, and using knowledge effectively in adult education (Engel 1992). This approach encourages students to actively seek knowledge rather than to passively receive information which is in keeping with the paradigm of information-knowledge-wisdom. In this continuum, information is presented to an individual and may be stored or discarded. If the individual retains the information, it may be converted into knowledge and possibly wisdom. Within this context, knowledge implies perception and understanding while wisdom denotes the elevated status of insight and accumulated learning. It is this paradigm—information-knowledge-wisdom–that forms the basis of all formal and informal education.

Research in educational psychology concerning adult learning has demonstrated that learning based on desired information, cumulative learning, incorporating concepts and ideas from a variety of disciplines as they relate to problem resolution, timely and appropriate feedback, and application of knowledge in a realistic situation enhance the knowledge acquisition process (Entwistle 1983). Problem-based learning curriculum is based on such research and comprises aspects of teaching and learning proven to be effective. Pure didactic teaching methodologies, on the other hand, assure that students are passive rather than active participants in the acquisition of knowledge. Limiting didactic instruction and promoting interactive, self-directed methods encourage students to synthesize information in a more meaningful way.

Utilizing a PBL curriculum, students are presented with problem situations and required to analyze the actions necessary to acquire relevant knowledge, skills, and attitudes needed to achieve resolution. Three principle objectives underlying problem-based learning are (1) the acquisition of a knowledge base, (2) the development of professional reasoning skills, and (3) the promotion of self-directed learning (Barrows 1985). With these goals in mind, a condition or question is introduced and the process begins. Twelve basic steps have been identified in this educational construct which include (1) problem identification and clarification, (2) problem analysis, (3) hypothesis(es) development, (4) requisite knowledge identification, (5) existing knowledge identification, (6) available resources identification, (7) information collection, (8) information synthesis and application to the problem, (9) repetition of previous steps as necessary, (10) knowledge deficit identification, (11) compilation and summary of what was learned, and (12) evaluation of understanding by applying new knowledge to another problem (Tedesco 1990). Following the PBL model, students learn to think and are more prepared to cope with future change. As a by-product of the knowledge acquisition process, students are exposed to the concepts underlying the skills and competencies necessary to perform in a practical setting. "PBL is an important means towards developing and maintaining creatively and critically reasoning practitioners who are well equipped to pursue self-directed learning throughout their professional life. Perhaps its most valuable attribute may prove to be that it can help to produce professionals capable of adapting to change and able to play an active role in change itself" (Engel 1992, 325).

Critical Thinking

Similar to problem-based learning is the concept of critical thinking. This involves reasoning and problem solving, and has been equated with the cognitive processes entailed in decision making, inquiry, or resolution. It implies reflection. Robert Ennis (1985, 45) defined critical thinking as "reflective and reasonable thinking that is focused on deciding what to believe or do." Richard Paul (1988, 49) determined it to be "the ability to reach sound conclusions based on observation and information." No matter how critical thinking is defined, however, the end result is an evaluative decision or action.

Critical thinking has been a goal of social studies education for some time and can be traced back at least as far as 1942 when it was the theme of the *Yearbook of the National Council for the Social Studies* (Patrick 1986). Widespread attention may be found at all levels of education in recent years, including various professional associations. Reason for interest in this topic where the education process is concerned would seem obvious. Critical thinking, however, may be growing in importance as employers demand graduates who possess the ability to think, analyze, and evaluate as evinced in the contents of current position vacancy descriptions.

While the skills involved in thinking critically may not be highly developed in all students as they begin graduate education programs, they may be nurtured in the classroom setting by presenting challenging questions similar to those typical of problem-based learning. Didactic teaching methods may be used to introduce tools or skills, with the intention that students ultimately are stimulated to think critically in order to resolve dilemmas or solve problems. By incorporating critical thinking into graduate school curriculum, students are prepared better to serve as tomorrow's practitioners. This may prove particularly true given the emerging ethical dilemmas accompanying advancing technologies.

Lifelong Learning

Complementary to problem-based learning and critical thinking is the philosophy of lifelong learning. "Lifelong learning emphasizes the need for renewal in learning over time" (Allen 1982, 68). The education process should not be viewed as something that ends with the receipt of a diploma or completion of a graduate degree. Few, if any, programs succeed in teaching students everything they must know upon entering the profession. Rather, motivation must be instilled to pursue continued learning throughout one's professional career and personal development. Education, in part, should strive to foster students' desires to seek new knowledge. In this manner, students will be more qualified to deal with change and the challenges the future holds.

Educational Recruitment

Admission standards for graduate education constitute part of a college or school's educational philosophy. The balance between admission standards, a school's existence, and the quality of education is complex. Admission standards influence enrollment. A school must maintain a high enough enrollment in order to justify its existence to senior administration. However, low admission standards can potentially hamper the quality of education. The perceived degree of excellence a program possesses directly affects recruitment. Although this intricate relationship mires educational recruitment, many disciplines have raised admission standards in order to strengthen the pool of graduates and influence the body of professionals.

EDUCATION FOR THE 21ST CENTURY PRACTITIONER

Given the continued adoption of emerging technologies and the changing nature of the profession, it would seem prudent to strengthen admission standards among schools of library and information studies in order to ensure successful future practitioners. The fact that future managers of information may very well hold primary membership in a profession other than library and information studies unless there is significant change in education also supports raising admission criteria (Braude 1993). This is not to say that one measure, such as the GRE score, should be the sole indicator of an individual's ability to function effectively in tomorrow's library or information center. Rather, a composite profile should be examined for each potential student. While the profile should not be limited to one measure, it must be representative of the individual's capabilities provided the direction the profession is moving toward.

Strengthening recruitment standards, though, will only address one issue concerning the preparation of practitioners for the 21st century. As stated earlier, current curriculum must be restructured to reflect evolving information infrastructures and the various complexities associated with the provision of information services. It must also encompass the future practitioners' potential role in the contents of information, not simply the management of the containers of information. This must be done within the context of the various areas of specialization in the profession as all will not be affected equally.

Restructuring the curriculum in schools of library and information studies requires a realistic, unbiased look at the profession and the information revolution occurring throughout society in order to design flexible programs that will produce effective future practitioners. Educational objectives must also allow for alternative career paths. It is imperative that the profession recognize new forms and structures of information, and begin to assimilate itself into the broader context of information (Braude 1993). This is not to say that education for work in a traditional library or information center setting should be discontinued, but that educational orientation must also account for the future. For as Jeng (1991, 116) has noted, "information professionals must possess theories and skills of state-of-the-art information technology in order to serve various information functions."

Under renovated programs, the core curriculum cannot be so

restrictive as not to allow for true specialization. A student who wishes to work in a health sciences information setting must be exposed to the theories underlying library and information studies, but should be allowed enough course work related to the area of specialization so that she/he is knowledgeable in that aspect of the field. Many of the topics taught in the traditional core can be incorporated into other courses, thus eliminating overlap. For instance, it is more logical for a student interested in health sciences information to take a class that focuses on management/administration issues specific to a health sciences setting rather than a general management course. Virtually the same information can be relayed to the student, but as it applies to the specific subject area. This would dispense with the general-to-specific subject approach currently employed in most programs. In this way, flexibility allows for breadth as well as depth.

All schools of library and information studies may not possess the capabilities to allow flexibility in every area of the field. Some may support a limited number of specializations. Others may opt for the "boutique" approach and remain highly concentrated concerning the line of endeavor they promote. Regardless of the breadth of the program offered by each individual college or school, though, course content must reflect trends in information services provision.

In addition to restructuring curriculum requirements, the content of course offerings needs to be re-evaluated based on the relationship between the profession and information in its broadest context. In light of advancing technologies, the profession–in order to remain competitive–must begin to address information content in addition to managing containers of information. It would not be prudent to maintain a reactive rather than proactive stance regarding information creation, storage, and dissemination given the variety of other professions currently encroaching upon the provision of information services. In addition, automation and technology need to be incorporated into classes wherever possible. Future practitioners have to understand the concepts underlying the emerging information infrastructure.

Course content can also be modified by incorporating such educational models and philosophies as problem-based learning, critical thinking, and lifelong learning. Utilizing these principles allows educators to present basic concepts and encourage students to explore and apply them on their own with the end result being graduates who can think and reason for themselves. Whether the theories supporting these teaching constructs are embraced in their entirety or not, programs that adopt aspects from each will produce students who are prepared more ably to cope with pending change.

Naturally, courses cannot cover every information technology application. Rather, the focus should be on the theories and concepts that underlie the application and using industry norms or standards where appropriate. In this way, common applications or systems become the vehicle to understanding the broader concept. For example, in seeking knowledge concerning the theories and concepts concerning electronic information retrieval, the student may be exposed to the process and various systems that support it. If a student comprehends database design, she/he will be able to retrieve information online via DIALOG, ondisc with a SilverPlatter CD-ROM, or from a personal database created using Pro-Cite. The differences in the retrieval process are negligible once the systems structure is understood since it then becomes a matter of learning a product or system-specific command and query language.

Still there remain many competencies that will not be included in formal classroom instruction but are required by the profession. These deficiencies may be offset by augmenting course work with practice through collaborative efforts between educators and practitioners. One method employed by many programs to accomplish this is through a field study or practicum. Students spend a designated number of hours working in a library or information center in exchange for course credit hours. These provide students with exposure to the realities of the profession and the application of information technologies employed in that particular setting. Another similar collaborative effort is that of mentoring programs. These may be formal or informal, and typically consist of a library/ information center or one of its professionals "adopting" a student or group of students. Again, these place the student in a work setting introducing her/him to the application of theory and technology. In light of the changing nature of the profession, the amount of information the profession expects students to be aware of, and the evolving information infrastructure, it would seem beneficial to strengthen collaborative efforts among educators and practitioners.

In keeping with the philosophy of lifelong learning, the importance of continuing education (CE) cannot be overstated. The information revolution continues after the classroom, and formal education should not be seen as the end of the learning process. Many topics needed to keep practitioners current regarding trends and technologies are appropriate for CE. Continuing education courses form an obvious link between state-of-the-art information and the practitioner in any profession in flux.

DISCUSSION

Given the changing nature of the profession and the impact of emerging technological applications, curriculum in schools of library and information studies must adapt to reflect the needs of future practitioners. This restructured curriculum–as does the current bevy of course offerings–will vary among programs. There most likely will continue to be dissent among educators and practitioners as to what should be the focus of that curriculum with the former stressing theory and the latter demanding skills and application. But as Vondran (1989, 30) states, "what both need in an environment of change is adaptable creative problem-solvers, who will soon develop into effective managers." In order to achieve this, however, students must be encouraged to think, analyze, evaluate, and apply while being exposed to technology as a vehicle to understanding. The educational environment for tomorrow's students must foster the desire to embrace emerging information infrastructures so as to produce successful 21st century information services providers.

REFERENCES

Allen, R. J. 1982. "New facts, assumptions, and approaches in American graduate education." In *Expanding the Missions of Graduate and Professional Education*, edited by F. Jacobs and R. J. Allen. San Francisco: Jossey-Bass, 1982.
Barrows, H. S. 1985. *How to design a problem-based curriculum for the preclinical years*. New York: Springer Publishing.

Braude, R. M. 1993. Impact of information technology on the role of health librarians. *Bulletin of the Medical Library Association* 81:408-13.

Creedy, D., Jan Horsfall, and Brian Hand. 1992. Problem-based learning in nurse education: An Australian view. *Journal of Advanced Nursing* 17:727-33.

Engel, C. E. 1992. Problem-based learning. *British Journal of Hospital Medicine* 48:325-29.

Ennis, R. H. 1985. A logical basis for measuring critical thinking skills. *Educational Leadership* 43:45-48.

Entwistle, N. J. 1983. *Styles of learning and teaching.* Chichester: John Wiley.

Jeng, L. H. 1993. From cataloging to organization of information: A paradigm for the core curriculum. *Journal of Education for Library and Information Science* 34:113-26.

Patrick, J. J. 1986. *Critical thinking in the social studies.* ERIC, ED 272 432.

Paul, R. 1988. Critical thinking in the classroom. *Teaching K-8* 18:49-51.

Stieg, M. F. 1992. *Change and challenge in library and information science education.* Chicago: American Library Association.

Stueart, R. D. 1989. "Educating Information Professionals for the 21st Century." In *2nd Pacific Conference, New Information technology for Library & Information professionals, Educational Media Specialists & Technologists,* edited by Ching-chi Chen and David I. Raitt, 389-94. West Newton, MA: MicroUse Information.

Tedesco, L. A. 1985. Responding to educational challenges with problem-based learning and information technology. *Journal of Dental Education* 54:544-47.

Vondran, R. F. 1990. Rethinking library education in the information age. *Journal of Library Administration* 11:27-36.

Reference Now and When

Margaret Morrison

DEEP SPACE

In the distant stardated future of the Starship Enterprise, the huge spaceship floats from world to world, ever expanding the knowledge of the universe. The crew of the ship represent different species, races, sexes, and mental capacities. And occupations. There are administrators, of course. There are engineers, a doctor and her medical staff, and a counsellor. There are a security officer and his staff, and there is at least one teacher. Although the role of cook seems to have been filled by the food "replicator," the ship even has a bartender. But there does not seem to be a librarian on the crew. While books often appear in crew members' offices and private quarters, they seem to be valued personal possessions, cherished antiques. For the provision of the information needed to conduct the business of the ship, there is the "computer," as in "Computer, get me all this decade's weather records for Rigel 4," or "Computer, how many dilithium crystals will we need to generate enough power to escape from orbit?" or even "Computer, play Beethoven's Ninth, this time with more woodwinds." This female-voiced computer stores, organizes, analyzes, retrieves, and customizes all sorts of information and can deliver the requested materials

Margaret Morrison is Head of the Reference and Access Services Department in the Health Sciences Library at the University of North Carolina, Chapel Hill, NC.

[Haworth co-indexing entry note]: "Reference Now and When." Morrison, Margaret. Co-published simultaneously in *Journal of Library Administration* (The Haworth Press, Inc.) Vol. 20, Nos. 3/4, 1995, pp. 131-140; and: *The Future of Information Services* (ed: Virginia Steel, and C. Brigid Welch) The Haworth Press, Inc., 1995, pp. 131-140. Multiple copies of this article/chapter may be purchased from The Haworth Document Delivery Center [1-800-3-HAWORTH; 9:00 a.m. - 5:00 p.m. (EST)].

immediately in any appropriate format. It obviously employs a natural language processor as its user interface and depends on sophisticated artificial intelligence programs to access its vast sources. Those sources, from ancient literary texts to the newest scientific readings, are all available in machine-readable form. The computer is never impatient, rude, judgmental, or wrong. It is, in short, the perfect reference librarian, the culmination of centuries of efforts to provide comprehensive information services to all.

Predictions of the metamorphosis of the reference librarian are undeniably premature; yet it is also undeniable that those who provide reference services, the sources they use, and the structure supporting them face enormous changes in a future far closer than that of the Enterprise.

BRIEF HISTORY OF REFERENCE SERVICES

The distant future has its roots in the recent past. Samuel Green formulated the first statement of personal assistance in libraries in 1876. Encouraging "personal intercourse and relations between librarians and readers," Green described his ideal reference librarian with the assurance and hauteur of a nineteenth century gentleman: "She must be a person of pleasant manners, and while of proper dignity, ready to unbend, and of a social disposition. It is well if there is a vein of philanthropy in her composition."[1] Francis Miksa and others place this formulation in the environment of the modern library movement, dedicated to developing the intellectual and moral faculties of the American citizenry, a tenet of the positivism of the time.[2] The educational role of reference librarians came to encompass bibliographic instruction in the early 1900s. The 1930s and '40s saw a concentration on improving reference sources, while the 1960s and '70s stressed interpersonal communications skills.[3]

For the past twenty-five years, computer technologies increasingly have defined the nature of reference services. Miksa portrays this situation as an extension of the information era that arose after World War II. Steig, tracing this evolution, points out that computers have made profound changes, not just in the services provided in libraries, but in the values underlying those services.[4] Among the changes she notes are increased and approved social isolation; a reduction in civility, especially in electronic mail and on bulletin boards; a reduction in a sense of job mastery, known as "deskilling;" and a greatly compressed and urgent sense of time. Most cogently, she describes the way automation can force unnatural conformity to non-human patterns:

> Many individuals who work with computers have so completely identified themselves with the machines that they have adopted the computer's standards. In all settings they insist on efficiency and speed and have little tolerance for ambiguity. They commonly display little understanding of their own feelings and lack empathy for others. The machine is perfect; humans should be no less.[5]

While this statement may imply more pathology than is evident among librarians, it is nonetheless clear that technology brings both benefits and liabilities to the reference process.

NEW MODELS OF REFERENCE SERVICE

In 1988, the University of Texas at Austin General Libraries undertook a series of programs focusing on the future of reference. Four of the library profession's most intrepid leaders have attempted to describe new models of reference services, and their visions are meant as much to challenge as to predict. Barbara Ford, then Associate Director of the Trinity University Library, opened the series with an investigation of the issues involved in providing services from a reference desk.[6] The presence of a reference desk, Ford related, promises services to everyone, but these services come with a relatively low common denominator. In addition to the critical issue of low-level and inefficient service, Ford cites the desk-related problems of burnout, changing user populations, and the introduction of new technologies, both fee-based and subsidized. Urging the re-examination of desk-based services, she considers such options as staffing an information desk with paraprofessionals or even with well-programmed computers; having library users make appointments with librarians for sophisticated assistance; and offering several configurations of remote services. Ford acknowledges the librarian's role as an advocate for users in complex technological and ethical environments, yet she insists that new visions for reference services are needed.

The following year the Future of Reference conference heard Francis Miksa, Professor in the Graduate School of Library and Information Science at the University of Texas, present a new paradigm of reference services.[7] Miksa began by sketching what he believes to be the current paradigm of collection-centered services, with acquisitions and cataloging making materials available, while reference assists with the interpretation of tools that point to the collections. In contrast to this model, Miksa posited a user-centered perspective:

> The information revolution . . . is not centered fundamentally on the types or numbers of knowledge records available, nor on the orientation of research, nor on the nature of the technology employed, although all of these factors play a role in it. Rather, the information revolution pivots on achieving specificity, on tailoring information retrieval to the specific information transfer requirements of users.[8]

In this user-centered paradigm, analysis of collections is less important than analysis of specific user needs; and reference services involve providing assistance with the analysis, management, and creation of information. The resulting environment places reference librarians among the user community outside of the library; the reference department becomes an administrative structure only, having no physical cohesion.

In 1990 Patricia Moholt, Associate Director of Institute Libraries at Rensselaer Polytechnic Institute, moved Miksa's theoretical user-centered model out of the realm of the metaphysical and placed it with startling clarity in the realm of the practical. Moholt described a system of Information Entrepreneurs.[9] These entrepreneurs, who used to be reference librarians, are charged $100 per hour to use the library, $100 per hour to use the online catalog, $25 per day per item loaned, and $10 per page plus royalties for photocopies. Other information services, presumably in this economic model, would be directly arranged with vendors. All other library users, except undergraduates, have to pay the same rates or contract with the entrepreneurs. In order to make a living, the information entrepreneurs have to identify potential clients, carefully analyze their needs, and provide specific and well-packaged results with great efficiency. For continuing success, the reference librarians have to show that their professional skills produce results markedly superior to those resulting from more amateur attempts.

Moholt's model echoes a number of the issues seen in Miksa's user-centered perspective. A close analysis of user needs, a movement toward specificity of information delivery, "deeper, fuller, and more accurate intellectual access to all information,"[10] and the placing of reference librarians outside of the library are common to both models. Moholt, who calls her economic model of library services "an imperfect exercise in imagination,"[11] nevertheless sees a great opportunity for reference librarians to participate in the design and delivery of information and information systems.

In 1991 Nancy Eaton, Dean of Library Services at Iowa State University, emphasized the impact of economics on the evolution of library and reference services. Eaton described a redesigned system of publishing and pricing practices, where the fixed costs of publishing, such as authorship and editorial activities, would be absorbed by the publisher, while the variable costs of printing and distribution would be passed on to decentralized facilities.[12] This distributed economic approach, while applicable to print products, is particularly suited to electronic information sources. Eaton sees the reference department as a collection of user workstations, with the librarian acting as an assistant to the user in navigating the systems and making educated choices. This position reflects the advocacy role that Ford saw so vital to the functions of the new reference librarian. Eaton, like Ford, believes that librarians must be active in the design of prototypes and research projects aimed to develop useful information creation and delivery systems.

Each of these writers is calling for fundamental alterations in the reference model—what kind of services are required, how specific those services are, who best performs those services, where those services are delivered, what tools are best used to provide the services, and how those services are to be administered. The front-line reference librarians who formally responded to each of the Future of Reference speakers tended to agree with the direction laid out. They expressed genuine concern about the pace of the changes being described and about the increased responsibilities on already burdened reference staffs. Yet from Tom Calvin's client-oriented reference librarians of 1975[13] through Charles Martell's client-centered academic libraries of 1983[14] to the Future of Reference conferences, voices for a dramatic shift in traditional reference patterns have been widely heard.

NEW REFERENCE STRUCTURES

With attention focused on user-centered services, reference librarians and reference departments will find themselves in structures very different from the hierarchical constructions common today. Reference resources, and all other information sources, will be increasingly automated; reference librarians will be better and more widely educated; and reference departments will become highly cooperative and minimally compartmentalized.

One of the most obvious changes in reference department structure involves the tools used to provide value-added, tailored reference services. While paper and microform and all current hard-copy sources of information will continue to exist and to be essential to research in some disciplines, more and more information will be available online or in other electronic forms. The vendors of direct online services show no sign of fading away; indeed there are more now than ever. And while the industry may see shifts in market targeting, diversification, and realignment, even a quick look at any of the library computing journals, and at many of the non-library computing journals, reveals a lively if adversarial vitality.[15]

CD-ROM and its offspring will be around for a while longer, delivering fixed-price alternatives to online searching. The 1987 edition of *CD-ROMs in Print* had 102 pages; the 1993 edition had grown to 736 pages and included relatively small sections on CD-I, multimedia, and electronic book products.[16] Even as the compact disk is portrayed as a temporary and interim medium, many signs point to its continuation for the next decade.[17]

Electronic primary publications are becoming increasingly available. A review of the *Directory of Electronic Journals, Newsletters and Academic Discussion Lists* lists 627 entries for 1991 (110 of which were journals or newsletters), 900 for 1992 (133 of which were journals or newsletters), and 1392 entries for 1993 (240 of which are journals or newsletters).[18] Fewer than fifty of these entries represent genuine electronic journals, but the trend toward electronic publication is strong. And the growth in the use of networks, even among those who cannot define network, is staggering. It seems clear that while the current databases, media, and networks may not be the same as the future databases, media, and networks, the growth of electronic information sources is unstoppable.

These electronic tools mean that the reference "desk" may be replaced by the reference "workstation." With good communications links, library users and reference staff may not actually need to see each other, although they will probably be able to do even that soon. Reference collections should shrink in size as more and more sophisticated sources are available, and preferable, locally or remotely, in electronic form. And the central geographic location that most reference departments occupy in the library building may no longer be as important as it is today. Instead, user workstations and associated advisory services will give the reference department its identity.

Certainly, new reference configurations will affect staffing. The ongoing development of computer-based assistance, ranging from good graphics to natural language capabilities and expert systems, will mean that the lower-level reference transactions and minimal service that concerned Ford will no longer require professional assistance, and that queries that exceed some well-defined threshold will be referred to a higher level. Paraprofessional staff, well-trained in communications skills rather than in clerical tasks, will negotiate most of the routine requests.

Librarians will take on new roles in analyzing user needs, manipulating and customizing all sorts of information, and designing improved access tools for broadly dispersed sources. While the renaissance-man, who knows something of everything, will continue to coexist with Green's philanthropic woman, these traditional values will find new expression in humane technologies. Reference librarians, many of whom now have advanced subject degrees in addition to the library science degree, may find that education in the processes of statistical and systems analysis, data management, and even graphic design is as useful as a love of Emily Dickinson or a fascination with quarks.

Jane Kleiner traces a recent trend in science and technology libraries that suggests that many libraries are centralizing services and collections as users are becoming more remote and decentralized.[19] Factors in this process of centralization include the financial advantages of consolidation and the technological possibilities of remote access. Kleiner cites a study by De Klerk and Euster that documents a need for increased professional and paraprofessional staff in reference departments to handle advances in automation.[20] Kleiner concludes that in the future there may be "fewer libraries staffed by librarians who are information professionals."[21] Kleiner's study should be tremendously reassuring to reference librarians faced with the isolation and competition of the reference models described by Ford, Miksa, and Moholt. The centralization of services and collections preserves the generous and civilizing values described by Steig, while the recognition of decentralized users reinforces the commitment to universal service.

The administrative structures of reference departments also have to respond to fundamental changes. Physically, reference collections may occupy much reduced space, and staff may be dispersed throughout the institution. Complex workstations will be widely distributed, and a well-educated staff will be available for assistance. With a premium on specialized services to users, reference departments will evaluate performance on criteria other than the number of questions answered, bibliographies prepared, or books reviewed. Management of the new reference department will be flatter, more cooperative, and more flexible than the hierarchical themes currently in place in most large libraries. While management theories change much more rapidly than libraries, less-structured administrations will be able to respond more quickly to technological, economic, and environmental shifts, giving more financial and institutional support to the reference process, which will in no way become less expensive as it becomes more complex and responsive.

ON TO STARDATE

The client-oriented model of reference services, with its emphasis on meeting the needs of the individual with customized information delivery, its reliance on automated information sources, and its promise of wide access, is only a few light years away from the Enterprise's "computer." But today's microchip is tomorrow's neural net. It may well be that the development of that extraordinary "computer" depends on reference librarians who become information managers who become expert system designers. In fact, the Starship Enterprise does not need reference librarians. They have become an integral and inseparable part of the future.

NOTES

1. Samuel S. Green, "Personal relations between librarians and readers," *Library Journal* (30 November 1876):74-81.
2. Francis Miksa, "The future of reference II: A paradigm of academic library organization," *College and Research Library News* (October 1989):784.
3. Barbara J. Ford, "The future of reference service," *College and Research Library News* (October 1988):578.
4. Margaret Steig, "Technology and the concept of reference or What will happen to the milkman's cow?" *Library Journal* (15 April 1990):48.
5. Steig, p. 48.
6. Ford, pp. 578-582.
7. Miksa, pp. 780-790.
8. Miksa, p. 785.
9. Patricia Moholt, "The future of reference III: A paradigm shift for information services," *College and Research Library News* (December 1990):1045-1051.
10. Moholt, p. 1050.
11. Moholt, p. 1048.
12. Nancy L. Eaton, "The future of reference IV: Document delivery and on-demand publishing: Implications for reference," *College and Research Library News* (September 1992):508-510.
13. Thomas J. Galvin, "The education of the new reference librarian," *Library Journal* (15 April 1975):727-730.
14. Charles R. Martell. *The Client-Centered Academic Library: An Organizational Model.* Westport, CT: Greenwood, 1983.
15. See the predatory cover of *Online* 17 (July 1993).
16. *CD-ROMs in Print.* Westport, CT: Meckler, 1987- .
17. Karl Beiser, "Ten myths about CD-ROM," *Online* 17 (November 1993):96-100.

18. Michael Strangelove, ed. *Directory of Electronic Journals, Newsletters, and Academic Discussion Lists.* 3 ed. Washington, DC: Association of Research Libraries, 1993.

19. Jane P. Kleiner, "The electronic library: The hub of the future's information networks," *Reference Librarian* 39 (-1993):131-139.

20. Ann De Klerk and Joanne R. Euster, "Technology and organizational metamorphoses," *Library Trends* 37 (Spring 1989):460-463.

21. Kleiner, p. 137.

Academic Partnership:
A Future for Special Collections

Stanley A. Chodorow
Lynda Corey Claassen

In June 1993, the Rare Books and Manuscripts Section of the Association of College and Research Libraries held a conference entitled, "Mainstream or Margin: How Others View Special Collections." Conference speakers included library directors, technical services administrators, and scholars, each giving his or her perspective on the issue. The general opinion seemed to be that Special Collections departments are or are tending to become more marginalized in the modern research library, and the speakers were concerned to tell the staff of those collections how to navigate back into the mainstream.

The advice took predictable paths. Library directors argued that Special Collections must serve the needs of the relevant–that is, local–community of faculty and students. One said that Special Collections departments must become more like other parts of the library: they need to expand their constituency among faculty and students, keep records of use, and put their catalogs online to adver-

---

Stanley A. Chodorow is Provost at the University of Pennsylvania at Philadelphia. He was formerly Dean, Arts and Humanities and Associate Vice Chancellor, Academic Planning at The University of California, San Diego. Lynda Corey Claassen is Head of the Mandeville Department of Special Collections, and Library Development Officer at the University of California, San Diego Libraries, San Diego, CA.

[Haworth co-indexing entry note]: "Academic Partnership: A Future for Special Collections." Chodorow, Stanley A., and Lynda Corey Claassen. Co-published simultaneously in *Journal of Library Administration* (The Haworth Press, Inc.) Vol. 20, Nos. 3/4, 1995, pp. 141-148; and: *The Future of Information Services* (ed: Virginia Steel, and C. Brigid Welch) The Haworth Press, Inc., 1995, pp. 141-148. Multiple copies of this article/chapter may be purchased from The Haworth Document Delivery Center [1-800-3-HAWORTH; 9:00 a.m. - 5:00 p.m. (EST)].

tise their collections. Another emphasized the centrality of Special Collections to the mission of the university at the same time that she noted their marginality in library planning and in the minds of many faculty, who are sure there are better uses for the resources devoted to the building and maintenance of Special Collections. She urged Special Collections librarians to integrate their planning into the library's general planning process and to advertise their collections to the faculty of their institutions by collecting materials of interest to faculty, by putting the catalog online, and so forth.

The technical services administrators described the problems Special Collections librarians face if they want to follow the advice of the library directors. One provided a list of advisables to improve service in Special Collections departments and, thereby, their appeal to the masses, such as they are in the academy: improve photocopy and other reprographic services; permit visiting scholars to use the collections after hours; increase interlibrary lending of materials, either through the lending of originals or copies of materials; prepare brief records for uncataloged materials; filter some material out of Special Collections into the general research collections. Another warned Special Collections librarians to mend their ways. He charged that Special Collections librarians often could not define what is or should be in Special Collections; that Special Collections facilities are expensive–the materials cost a lot, the search for them costs a lot, processing and preservation cost a lot. For him, the best approach to the "problem" of Special Collections is for them to be defined into a smaller estate, to find a way to fit within the systems that organize the rest of the library, and to expand their usefulness to the "average" user.

Finally, the scholars offered testimonials to the importance of Special Collections, but they also offered a couple of suggestions. One suggested the improvement of reprographic services and the collection of current, "popular culture" materials for the benefit of future scholars. The other suggested that Special Collections librarians "use the users" of their materials to help create reference tools that would enhance the utility of the collections.

The main point of all the speakers at the conference was that Special Collections librarians should increase the visibility of their collections and their service to the campus community. But the speakers did not really address how Special Collections librarians might accomplish these goals. This article begins a discussion of some ways this problem might be tackled, largely through a change in attitude and values. While many others have addressed, and will continue to address how/when/if the latest information technologies will affect special collections, we turn to an exploration of "academic partnering"–a means to help move Special Collections into the mainstream.

In the future, Special Collections can only be vital to the academic community of a campus if they contain materials relevant to the scholarship and instructional activities of the faculty and students of that campus. The difficulty is that materials collected today because of the energetic interest of a group of faculty can be rendered marginal tomorrow by the changing interests or composition of that faculty. Many Special Collections Departments have a few active and several inactive parts of their collections, and many librarians of such collections have had the experience of dedicating long years and many dollars to build a particular corpus of material only to find it derelict on the rocks of the academic geography of their university sometime after the corpus reaches maturity. Consequently, much of the activity in Special Collections departments appears to be unrelated to the current interests of the faculty and students.

What is to be done? The first thing to do is to try to link collecting activities to long-term commitments by the university administration to support the programs for which the collecting is being done. We have tended to treat Special Collections departments as treasure houses, rather than academic resources, and one collects treasures for their market value, not necessarily their academic value.[1] This orientation has produced the strange situation that was the implicit problem of the RBMS conference: we spend significant resources on collections that, having little or nothing to do with current or planned academic interests of the campus, are actually an expensive gift made by the university to outsiders–to either local "non-primary clientele" or to the international community of scholars. When we notice this kind of use of our shrinking resources, we raise the questions addressed at the conference.

The only way to avoid this anomaly is to coordinate the building of Special Collections with academic planning in the same way as the general research collections are constructed in the library. Special Collections librarians must look upon their collections as academic resources, not precious stones, and must manage them with reference to the development of the academic programs of their universities. This might even mean the careful "transfer" of materials when the academic program takes a decisive and permanent turn away from its traditional course. Such "transfers" should be done in a way that favors the movement of the affected materials to a library that already has a significant related collection, where an appropriate context for the collection is available.

The tendency to treat the materials in Special Collections as treasures–as museum pieces–has not only led us to collect and hold what is not relevant to the academic programs of the university but has also caused us to protect them, both by making them difficult to use and by restraining any impulse toward sharing them. One does not share precious possessions, especially if the sharing might diminish their value.

But academic values emphasize sharing. Scientists share strains of bacteria; social scientists share data; humanists share written and artistic materials, rare and common. Moreover, sharing has become a critical element of modern library management: as resources continue to decline, shared access to materials through technology increases in importance. The definition of a collection is no longer what is owned by a particular library but what that library can make available to its clientele–except in Special Collections. There, the old possessiveness remains strong, and scholars interested in a topic must find and visit their materials where they are–an arduous, time-consuming, and expensive process.

In the future, Special Collections departments must make themselves more useful to the faculty and students on their campuses by linking themselves–electronically and intellectually–to other collections that have similar materials. They need to become entry points not just to specific items owned at that particular location but to the whole corpus of materials relevant to the scholars who might use what they own. They can help create "virtual special collections." Only then will scholars treat them as more than repositories, to be visited, exploited, and then abandoned for other pastures.

But Special Collections have what they have, and they cannot just go out and remake themselves to fit the current contours of local academic programs. They can, however, direct more focus on their client group (i.e., their users) to establish or re-establish strong academic partnerships. Thus, Special Collections librarians may take several approaches to reconnecting with the academic program. First, they can work with faculty to develop "programs" for undergraduates that lead to research projects in Special Collections. Use of the materials often requires special skills and knowledge–linguistic and intellectual–that take time to develop. Working together, faculty and librarians can design programs of courses to acquire those skills and offer to students, as a reward for following the program, the opportunity to work with the rare materials in the collections. Brochures or broadsheets explaining these programs should be distributed to students when they enter the university and should be available in departmental offices and other places where students come for academic information and counseling.

Second, librarians should take advantage of faculty mentor programs and student research programs to bring students into their collections. Librarians need to find only a few faculty willing to cooperate in such programs to populate their reading rooms with students.

Special collections librarians may offer students more than the opportunity to work with unique materials and more than help in using those materials. They should ask for help, as well as give help. For example, graduate students (or exceptional undergraduates) who have appropriate language abilities and subject expertise can be incorporated into the research, selection, and catalog components of major exhibitions. The students then become intellectual resources for Special Collections, and a significant symbiotic relationship is established. Yes, the librarian must be available to supervise and give direction, but the rewards for both student and librarian far outweigh any perceived negatives. The same level of student assistance can also be useful in doing "fieldwork" for collection development, or in the compilation of bibliographies, indexes, or desiderata lists. Faculty are generally enthusiastic about the opportunity for their students to participate in "real life" situations that provide both meaningful intellectual exercise and "job experience." Depending on the assignment, students may earn either academic credit or hourly wages. Special Collections can help tomorrow's scholars become the once and future users of their materials.

Faculty do understand that scholars need reference tools for the collections, and their students can also assist in the creation of those tools. Again, Special Collections librarians should "use their users." Librarians should make participation in the creation of reference databases for their collections an expectation of users, student and faculty alike. The opportunity to contribute something to the collection–to add value to it–will be a powerful attraction to students to take advantage of the programs that lead to use of the collections. For most of their education, students are recipients of assistance and instruction; it is one of the elements of their situation that keeps them from fully maturing. Special Collections can offer them the opportunity to give back something of value to the library and the university community–additional information about special resources that will have value to other students and scholars.

The databases or tools that might be created would provide information about persons, places, events, and subjects mentioned in the materials held in Special Collections. They might also provide guidance to libraries where similar materials can be found; the libraries could then build an effective electronic network to help users gain access to what they need. Special digitization or hypertext projects that feature and/or expand special collections materials might also be created. These additions to Special Collections would alone increase markedly the service they provide to users, but they might also lead to a truly cooperative attitude among libraries. In fact, the development of "linked" Special Collections through electronic networks, reference databases, and ILL would be a return to scholarly conditions that existed in Europe before World War II. At that time, libraries often loaned materials, including medieval manuscripts, to other libraries for use by local scholars. Published catalogs made the contents of the various major collections known, even if many of the catalogs were defective. Now, the electronic revolution permits us to recreate those friendly conditions and to improve on them. The identification of rare materials is often the work of highly trained scholars. We need to put such scholars and their students to work on our collections and to capture in our electronic environment what they have to tell us about unknown or misconstrued elements of our special collection.

Collections need daily use to maintain their animation. Users are the life-givers of collections, and the future of Special Collections demands that users play a more vital role on our stage. Users generate both the need and the justification for continued acquisitions, and they shape those acquisitions around intellectual programs. Without constant use, collections may have a memory of past life but no actual life, and therefore no promise. A strategy to connect Special Collections with academic programs and with one another is essential to save them from becoming tombs.

A community of users not only sustains the life of the collection but also sustains the life of scholarship. It is a medium of exchange, an instrument of education, an improver of individual scholars. A medievalist who spends a great deal of time using collections at the Vatican, the Bibliotheque National, or the British Library becomes a better medievalist and contributes to the quality of the collection. Users inform the librarians and each other about the contents of the library and help the librarians recognize the gaps in their holdings and the relationship between their library and others in which related materials can be found.

To create the whole animal—the collection animated by a specific community of readers—one must have a collection good enough to attract and sustain that community. This means that, from the scholar's point of view, there should be a tendency toward consolidation of collections in various fields. The presidential libraries are an apt, if insoluble, example of the problem. To work on more than one president, a scholar has to traipse all over the country, an expensive and ridiculous situation, from the scholar's point of view. We urge Special Collections librarians to consider consolidating collections, through trades, deposits, or any other means, when feasible, and to link and share related collections when actual consolidation is impossible. A rich collection can sustain generations of scholars; it is unlikely to become a dilapidated monument on the academic landscape of a campus.

As a practical matter—because trades, acquisitions, and deposits are unlikely to unite collections in specific fields—the achievement of this goal requires the creation of online catalogs and digital images of as much material as possible, especially where there is a cooperative effort of several libraries to create a common resource.

In the end, the centrality–the "mainstream-ness"–of Special Collections will depend not only on how well they are accommodated to the library's regular systems or on their relationship with the general collections, but on their importance to the academic programs. The best allies of Special Collections librarians and the supporters of the collections themselves are the faculty, administrators, and students. Special Collections librarians should not confine themselves to acts of persuasion within the library walls; they should work with academics, from the chief academic officer of the campus on down, to generate users for their collections and for the collections that could be accessed through them. Special Collections librarians should be ambassadors of their collections and services. But ambassadors do not stay home; they are posted to foreign ports. In this case, the ports are the academic programs of the university, where librarians traffic with the resident faculty and students.

NOTE

1. For a brief but cogent history of the transition from "treasure house" to "special collections," see: William L. Joyce, "The Evolution of the Concept of Special Collections in American Research Libraries," *Rare Books & Manuscripts Librarianship* 3 (Spring 1988):19-29.

Future Directions
for Government Information

Linda M. Kennedy

Access to federal information is changing dramatically as a result
of Clinton administration policies, federal budget cuts, technological changes, and user demand. Much more information is being
distributed electronically, particularly in online formats. Computer-
literate federal information users are obtaining electronic information directly. In the new electronic environment, government
information will be available from a diversity of sources–commercial, public and private–including federal depository libraries.[1]
Library organization of services, and the Depository Library Program are also changing as a result of some of the same factors
affecting federal government information.

Of concern to libraries, especially in regard to federal government information, is democracy of access to government information. Many users, those with the expertise, time and equipment to
use online electronic resources, are accessing government information. However, if information is available only in an electronic
format, it is essential that any user be able to obtain access. Depository libraries and community information networks can provide
assistance and access to those who lack the resources to access

Linda M. Kennedy is Head of the Government Documents Department,
Shields Library, University of California, Davis. She is a past chair of the Government Documents Round Table of the American Library Association and is currently a member of the Depository Library Council to the Public Printer.

[Haworth co-indexing entry note]: "Future Directions for Government Information." Kennedy,
Linda M. Co-published simultaneously in *Journal of Library Administration* (The Haworth Press, Inc.)
Vol. 20, Nos. 3/4, 1995, pp. 149-165; and: *The Future of Information Services* (ed: Virginia Steel, and C.
Brigid Welch) The Haworth Press, Inc., 1995, pp. 149-165. Multiple copies of this article/chapter may
be purchased from The Haworth Document Delivery Center [1-800-3-HAWORTH; 9:00 a.m. - 5:00
p.m. (EST)].

federal electronic information directly. Even for those who have the resources, depository librarians can assist in locating information. The establishment of community free-nets (community-based networks offering a variety of information resources and services) offer tremendous potential for increasing access to local and state information resources, as well as helping expand access. Libraries, including depository libraries, need to be part of the planning and implementation of community-based information networks, providing expertise in organization and access to information resources. Full access to the Internet through such networks will be limited until affordable universal access is achieved through implementation of the national information infrastructure, along with appropriate telecommunications industry regulation. Mechanisms for ensuring continued free access to federal information resources through depository libraries to the diversity of federal agency resources must also be developed.

ADMINISTRATION INITIATIVES

The Clinton Administration has introduced a number of major policy documents which emphasize development of a National Information Infrastructure (NII), "a seamless web of communications networks, computers, databases, and consumer electronics . . . Development of the NII will help unleash an information revolution that will change forever the way people live, work and interact with each other."[2] Although information is identified as one of the nation's most critical resources and the government has a key leadership role, the Administration assumes that the private sector will build and run virtually all of the National Information Infrastructure (NII). With commercial use already changing the nature of the Internet, public interest groups such as library organizations ask whether access to the NII will depend upon one's economic status or information access skills. The communications reform legislation required to govern the new NII will need to not only facilitate private sector infrastructure development but also promote the social goals outlined in the Clinton policy documents.

President Clinton's technology initiative, *Technology for America's Economic Growth, A New Direction to Build Economic Strength,*[3] introduced on February 22, 1993, indicated the importance the new administration placed on information technology. While he was in the Senate, Vice-President Gore introduced the High Performance Computing and Act of 1991; its passage funded research and development for more powerful supercomputers, faster computer networks and the first national high speed network (the National Research and Education Network, or NREN). Clinton's technology initiative further implements and funds the high-performance computing and communications program, including NREN, creates an information infrastructure technology program and a Task Force on Information Infrastructure, funds pilot projects through the National Telecommunications and Information Administration (part of the Department of Commerce) and promotes dissemination of federal information through the Internet/NREN.

The Administration also acted quickly to make its own information available electronically.[4] Using an experimental system developed during the presidential campaign, the White House began distributing electronic versions of press releases to a variety of online services and discussion groups, such as USENET and CompuServe. Individuals can also sign up directly to receive the press releases. Major documents, such as the text of the *National Performance Review* were distributed first electronically. White House documents are now ubiquitous on the Internet, where they form a staple of most freenets and gophers. The Administration also established Internet mail addresses for communicating with the White House, to either the President or Vice-President. (Unfortunately, the White House does not yet have the capability to respond via electronic mail.) Pilot projects for communicating electronically with the Senate and House are also under development.

The potential for increased participation in the development of public policy through electronic communication with elected officials and through electronic "town hall meetings" is enormous. The lobbying impact of computer users is also expanding. Recent successes in gaining access to electronic Securities and Exchange Commission (SEC) filings and the recent passage in California (after heavy lobbying of the Legislature by computer users) of a bill to make bills and bill status available electronically are an indication of the potential clout of the computer-literate population.

On September 15th, 1993 President Clinton introduced *The National Information Infrastructure: Agenda for Action.*[4] Nine principles and goals guide the development of policy initiatives for the NII:

- Promote private sector investment
- Extend the "universal service" concept to ensure that information resources are available to all at affordable prices
- Act as a catalyst to promote technological innovation and new applications
- Promote seamless, interactive, user-driven operation of the NII
- Ensure information security and network reliability
- Improve management of the radio frequency spectrum
- Protect intellectual property rights
- Coordinate with other levels of government and with other nations
- Provide access to government and improve government procurement

The Information Infrastructure Task Force (IITF), created by Executive order in September 1993, began work quickly "to articulate and implement the Administration's vision for the NII."[5] A high-level group of cabinet officers headed by Department of Commerce Secretary Ron Brown, the IITF also established working groups to deal with problematic aspects of policy, such as communication privacy, for the national information superhighway. An Advisory Council on the National Information Infrastructure was appointed in January 1994 to advise the Secretary on matters related to the development of the NII. Its twenty-five members include one librarian, Toni Carbo Bearman, library school dean and former Executive Director of the National Commission on Libraries and Information Science.

TELECOMMUNICATIONS POLICY REFORM

Development and deployment of the NII will be led by the private sector, but "carefully crafted government action will complement and enhance the efforts of the private sector and assure the growth of an information infrastructure available to all Americans at reasonable cost."[6] The existing regulatory framework approaches telephone, television, cable and other telecommunications media separately; competition is carefully controlled. On January 11, 1993, Vice-President Albert Gore announced the administration's proposals for telecommunications policy revision and released an *Administration White Paper on Communications Act Reforms.*[7] That document states that "it is a goal of this Administration that by the year 2000 all of the classrooms, libraries, hospitals and clinics in the United States will be connected to the NII." The Administration's proposal focuses on five principles: (1) encourage private investment, (2) promote and protect competition, (3) provide open access to the network, (4) avoid creating a society of information haves and have-nots, and (5) encourage flexibility.

This is a critical period of policy development, since major revisions to the Communications Act of 1934 are likely to pass this year. Public interest groups need to act quickly to articulate concerns and ensure that legislation provides adequate safeguards to ensure equitable access to the NII. In September, 1993, representatives of fifteen national library and information organizations met in Washington, D.C. to discuss the critical policy issues dealing with the implementation of the NII and to develop a consensus on key principles to be used to guide its development. The Telecommunications and Information Infrastructure Policy Forum[8,9] identified key principles in the following areas: First Amendment and Intellectual Freedom, Privacy, Intellectual Property, Ubiquity, Equitable Access and Interoperability. Among the points made: Access to basic network services should be affordable and accessible to all; resources must be allocated to provide basic public access. This concept of universal service, which has characterized telephone service in this country, must become part of our expectations for the new communications environment. Clinton Administration policy statements stress the goal of universal service and this concept is included in many of the telecommunications policy draft legislation. Defining universal service and deciding who will pay for the guarantee of universal service is the topic of hearings being held in locations around the country by the National Telecommunications and Information Administration.

FEDERAL INFORMATION POLICY

Federal information policy has been a battle ground for the past decade. Competing stakeholder groups–library organizations, the information industry, public interest groups–have attempted to influence government policy.

Following a federal information policy revision process which began in 1987, the Office of Management and Budget (OMB) issued a major revision of its Circular A-130, "Management of Federal Information Resources."[10] The revision, which became effective June 25, 1993, incorporated new policies for managing government information that encouraged agencies to use electronic information to improve public access. Agency electronic products would be governed by the same policies that apply to printed or audiovisual products. Agencies are to develop indexes to help the public locate government information. In pricing information products, agencies should recover only those costs associated with the dissemination of information, not the costs of its creation or collection. Contrary to past policy, the OMB states that "as a matter of policy, electronic dissemination products generally should be provided to the depository libraries."[15] The costs associated with distribution are a consideration in making decisions about whether to distribute electronic information through the depositories, OMB asserts.

LESS INFORMATION

While library organizations have had some success in influencing federal information policies to increase access to government information, other factors are working to reduce availability. Efforts to trim the federal budget to reduce the deficit and to cut or reallocate expenditures are accelerating in Congress. Library programs such as the Library Services and Construction Act (LSCA) which help support connectivity improvements for libraries have already been targeted for elimination in the 1995 budget. Several cost-cutting measures circulating in the 103rd Congress propose 7.5% reductions for Legislative Branch appropriations, which will significantly affect the Depository Library Program in GPO and the Library of Congress. The National Performance Review (NPR)[12,13] headed by Vice-President Gore placed a great deal of emphasis on the possibilities of information technology to save money and improve services, from facilitating government contracting and procurement, to delivering government services and providing access to government information. Unfortunately, its recommendations involving the Government Printing Office were not well received by the library community. Government printing would be decentralized, with agencies contracting out their own printing. Agencies would disseminate their own publications to the depository libraries, a patently unworkable scheme. Draft legislation implementing the NPR recommendations is pending in Congress. The version which passed the House of Representatives does retain the centralized printing functions of the Government Printing Office in the Legislative Branch. It also transfers the administration of the Depository Library Program to the Library of Congress.

Multiple factors, including federal budget cuts, the Paperwork Reduction Act and other federal information policies have combined to make federal information less available over the years.[14] Agencies reduce information collection and dissemination operations, increase prices for information products or transfer information products to the private sector. The process of privatization usually removes titles from the depository library program and increases the price to the user.

As a result of past administration policies, control of government databases was sometimes relinquished to contractors. For example, the National Technical Information Service (NTIS) does not own the NTIS bibliographic database. The Department of Justice's JURIS database of court decisions was shut down by the contractor when pressures mounted to make the federal case law material, which had been copyrighted by the vendor, available to the public. An impressive victory, however, was won last year when the Securities and Exchange Commissions announced that its EDGAR database of financial filings from public companies would be made available over the Internet–data formerly available only at high costs from commercial vendors.[15] Pressure from library organizations also reversed a decision of the Department of Education to allow the ERIC database to be copyrighted by the vendor.

Agencies may also transfer their information dissemination functions to the National Technical Information Service. As a self-supporting organization, NTIS prices are high. Data products in particular are expensive, since they are priced to recover costs and the market for an individual title may be limited.

AGENCY DEVELOPMENTS AND COMPETITION

There have been a number of positive developments in access to federal electronic information. The Library of Congress significantly enhanced in access to federal electronic information through the creation of its LOCIS and LC MARVEL systems. Each is available by dial-in and through the Internet. The Library of Congress Information System (LOCIS) accesses more than 26 million records in files such as the LC Catalog, copyright files, and federal legislative bills and status. The Library of Congress Machine-Assisted Realization of the Virtual Electronic Library (LC MARVEL) is an extensive gopher accessing a diverse array of government information resources from many agencies. The Department of Commerce has operated its Economic Bulletin Board, a rich resource of timely economic data, for several years. Use increased dramatically when it became available on the Internet in late 1993, at first free on an experimental basis, and then for a modest cost.

FedWorld, operated by the National Technical Information Service, has more than 35,000 registered users, and is expanding to accommodate as many as 200 simultaneous users. Billed as "the government's electronic marketplace for information," FedWorld is accessible through the Internet or telephone line. FedWorld serves as a gateway to more than 100 federal bulletin boards. NTIS has placed a high priority on making important documents, such as the *Health Security Plan,* available for downloading (for a fee) within hours of their release. Online orders and downloads can be billed to a credit card or deposit account.

The Government Printing Office Electronic Information Access Enhancement Act of 1993 (PL 103-40), enacted in June of 1993, is in the process of implementation. Under the GPO Access Act, the Superintendent of Documents will maintain an electronic directory or locator of federal electronic information, provide online access to the *Congressional Record, Federal Register* and other appropriate publications, and operate an electronic storage facility for federal information. The GPO Access system will be free to federal depository libraries, and priced at the incremental cost of dissemination to other users.

The American Technology Pre-eminence Act of 1991 requires all federal agencies to submit to NTIS unclassified scientific, technical and engineering information (STEI) resulting from federally funded research and development activities. Implementing regulations published in the *Federal Register*[16] in January 1993 make the clarification that the new procedures in no way relieve libraries of their responsibilities for distributing publications through the Depository Library Program. NTIS also promises to provide depository libraries online access to a listing of STEI products, a mechanism for obtaining copies of material they have not received, and, "as soon as practical," a system of full-text access at no charge to the libraries or the issuing agency, provided that online access to the list of STEI products is "restricted to the Library and its staff and that the full-text products . . . are available only to the community served by that Library."[17] While an exciting development, the regulations raise a number of questions about placing conditions on access to uncopyrighted government information in depository libraries. Also, NTIS promulgated the regulations without consultation with the Government Printing Office and consideration of GPO Access as a potential STEI gateway for the depository libraries.

GPO and NTIS are essentially competing to gain precedence in providing access to federal information in electronic formats. NTIS, because of its position within the Department of Commerce, and because its director is a member of the Information Infrastructure Task Force, is well-situated to influence policy. The Government Printing Office, because of depository library traditions and the

GPO Access Act's commitment to low-cost electronic access and free access through depository libraries, has support from many librarians and library organizations. OMB's government information locator concept, discussed below, emphasizes a diversity of access points and agency-based directories. A decentralized approach to electronic information access is likely to characterize access to electronic federal information as opposed to the centralized distribution model which characterizes the distribution of printed products and tangible electronic products through the Depository Library Program.

FEDERAL DEPOSITORY LIBRARY PROGRAM

As stated in OMB Circular A-130, "Depository libraries are major partners with the Federal Government in the dissemination of information and contribute significantly to the diversity of information resources available to the public. They provide a mechanism for wide distribution of government information that guarantees basic information to the public."[19] The contributions of the federal depository library program to long-term access to federal government information should not be underestimated. Through this mechanism, important government documents and reference works are distributed across the United States to every Congressional district. (Each Congressional district may have up to two depository libraries, in addition to law libraries; there are more than 1400 depository libraries.) Libraries provide both bibliographic access and preservation for government information. With large documents collections, a core of expertise exists to assist with locating information and making referrals within the federal bureaucracy. The Government Printing Office catalogs on OCLC all documents distributed, and also prepares the *Monthly Catalog of United States Government Publications* to be distributed in print and microfiche formats. All monographic titles receive individual cataloging.

The nationwide trend of conversion of documents processing from manual to online, and the integration of documents holdings into the library online catalogs, is greatly increasing use of documents, and providing analytics for titles which would otherwise not receive individual cataloging. The tremendous subject range of government information increases the depth of a library's research holdings. Analytics for NASA and Department of Energy reports, for example, illuminate an area of "grey literature" which does not usually receive access through library catalogs, except through separate technical report databases.

Many libraries are utilizing automatic tapeloads of GPO cataloging via commercial vendors which allows them to expedite processing and reduce processing staffs. Reducing processing staff may also mean "mainstreaming" separate government information processing units into other library technical processing units. Yet another trend, in this period of rapidly diminishing library resources, is the elimination of separate documents reference desks. Theoretically, when change is creatively managed, with the full involvement of the staff concerned, adequate service to government information can be preserved. Cross-fertilizations, such as business and government information, or social sciences and government information, could even improve service when adequate staffing and training is provided. Government documents reference involves many specialized aspects, such as the location of treaties, laws, regulations, and Supreme Court Cases, or finding technical report literature. It also means dealing with CD-ROMs, microfiche and maps. Many printed or electronic reference sources, such as the United States census and foreign trade data, require an understanding of publication patterns, organization or specialized classification schemes. It would be useful to evaluate the extent to which government information expertise has been extended to the general reference staff when reference desks have merged, or whether specialized expertise has simply been lost.

The experience and insights brought to government information reference librarians by the deluge of electronic information, especially CD-ROM, has provided a number of unexpected benefits. Government information librarians have been challenged, exasperated, and excited by the many new CD-ROM databases which can be received through the depository program. The documents unit was often the first library unit to deal with electronic information on this level. Unlike commercial bibliographic databases which libraries had been acquiring, the government CD-ROMs did not have standard software interfaces, and were often non-bibliographic, either numeric databases such as the 1990 Census disks, or mixed textual and numeric data bases such as the National Trade Data Bank (NTDB). Each agency pursues its own approach to software, and the results are mixed regarding user friendliness–learning enough about each of the databases to assist users is a major challenge. Many depository librarians met the challenge of electronic information, becoming innovative and flexible in providing public service to these resources, and gaining a great deal of technical expertise in the process. They have had to develop new models of public service as well, determining their limits of service in providing access to information. Besides computer users of increasing sophistication who are eager to download data to manipulate and edit, they also serve users without expertise. Also, certain databases are distributed without software; libraries have had to decide how (and whether) to provide access, for example, to Department of Commerce databases such as the *American Housing Survey,* or the *Current Population Survey* which require statistical programs such as SASS or SPSS. In many cases, new campus relationships have also been forged. In large academic institutions, links with the computing center or other units using statistical packages or geographical information systems (GIS) have been established, making use of technical expertise and equipment not available in the library. In the near future, another challenge awaits depository libraries: the receipt of increasingly sophisticated GIS data products.

Again, often ahead of traditional reference units, government information librarians have had to expand their horizons to include assistance in locating government information on gophers and ftp sites through the Internet. Because so many major documents are available online long before the arrival of the printed edition, it has become a natural extension of government information reference to locate and download reports of high interest, or to assist users in locating them.

RESTRUCTURING THE DEPOSITORY LIBRARY PROGRAM

The disparity among depository libraries in their ability to take advantage of electronic information is great. Large public or academic libraries have been able to devote the staff and resources necessary to provide access. Small libraries have often not acquired electronic products, or if they have acquired them, have not provided adequate access. This disparity is of great concern to depository librarians and the Government Printing Office.

Various models for restructuring the depository library program are being developed to address problems of uneven resources and service among depositories, the ongoing budget shortfalls of the Government Printing Office, and changes in technology and distribution patterns for government information. "Alternatives for Restructuring the Depository Library Program,"[20] prepared in 1993 by the Depository Library Council to the Public Printer, included the model of a tiered arrangement of multiple service levels: basic, intermediate and full. This concept was originally introduced by the Association for Research Libraries Task Force on Government Information in Electronic Format in 1988. The Council is also exploring greater use of resource sharing arrangements. Many of these changes will require changes to the laws governing the Depository Library Program.

In April of 1993, a small group of depository librarians gathered together in Washington to begin the consensus building process for restructuring the depository library program. The Dupont Circle Group, as they came to be known, circulated discussion drafts[21] widely in the community. Their work resulted in the Chicago Conference on the Future of Government Information held in Chicago in October, 1993, at which more than 160 government information specialists gathered to launch a grass-roots effort to ensure equitable public access to government information in all formats as a cornerstone of the NII. The group defined the basic mission and characteristics of a depository library program that could be used to formulate and evaluate legislation.[22]

ACCESS AND PRESERVATION ISSUES

Important challenges remain in accessing government information online through the Internet and other parts of the information infrastructure. First, guiding the user to the full range of federal information resources, including unique resources only available in print. Part of the problem will be addressed by the full development of government information locators. The Office of Management and Budget has proposed development of an agency-based Government Information Locator Service (GILS).[18] Each agency would develop its own locator, using standards that promote interoperability of search and retrieval mechanisms, network communications, user identification, document identifiers, etc. The public would access the GILS directly or through intermediaries such as the GPO, NTIS or public libraries and private information services. A variety of media would provide access to GILS: kiosks, fax, 800 numbers, electronic mail, bulletin boards and offline media such as printed publications and diskettes.

Government information access will also benefit from improvements in bibliographic access through the Internet. Veronica and Archie access, while helpful, is time-consuming and inexact. Librarians and library organizations need to become much more fully involved in improving bibliographic access to networked information.

Yet another concern is preservation of federal information available in online and other formats. Currently, important resources such as the *Federal Register* and *Weekly Compilation of Presidential Documents,* and other Congressional and executive agency publications, receive bibliographic access and preservation in depository libraries around the nation. Although the Center for Electronic Records at the National Archives is beginning to bring some organization to the task of preserving and providing access to federal electronic records, adequate mechanisms for continued access and preservation for online information have not yet been developed. Information currently residing on gophers and at ftp sites will not be maintained for the long-term. CD-ROM and floppy disk formats also present challenges, since the equipment, operating systems, and software needed to access the databases may not be available ten or twenty years in the future. A mechanism for locating and delivering all electronic government information electronically will need to be developed to compensate for the fact that information is no longer distributed around the nation and preserved for posterity, as with printed material. It may also be necessary for research libraries to develop their own electronic archives. *Presidential*

Papers of past Administrations are still used frequently by research-ers–it would be ironic if the speeches of President Clinton and Vice-President Gore, who have done so much to increase electronic access to government information, were lost to future generations.

The ubiquitous availability of some government information in online formats such as on gophers, bulletin boards and community free-nets is significantly changing the way users perceive govern-ment information. More and more users use government informa-tion directly, gaining an intimate familiarity with Presidential press releases and speeches, the full text of important documents such as the North American Free Trade Agreement, or economic informa-tion such as that available on the Economic Bulletin Board. Federal information is less mysterious, more accessible to the common man or woman, including those who do not use libraries. Regardless of the organizational structure of a library, it will be essential to provide access to increasingly high profile federal information resources.

The ability to provide access to electronic information is essen-tial for every library, not only depository libraries. It is absolutely critical, if libraries are to survive and to meet the information needs of their clientele, to provide access to the full range of information. Information, especially federal information, is making an inevitable transition from print to electronic formats, and libraries without the ability to use electronic formats will provide access to a diminishing range of information.

NOTES

1. Office of Technology Assessment, *Making Government Work; Electronic Delivery of Federal Services* (OTA-TCT-578) (Washington, D.C., GPO, 1993).

2. Information Infrastructure Task Force, *The National Information Infra-structure: Agenda for Action* (Washington, D.C., Executive Office of the Presi-dent, 1993): 3.

3. Clinton, Bill. *Technology for America's Economic Growth: A New Direc-tion to Build Economic Strength* (Washington, D.C., GPO, 1993).

4. Information Infrastructure Task Force, *The National Information Infra-structure: Agenda for Action*.

5. Ibid, 19.

6. Ibid, 3.

7. *Administration White Paper on Communications Act Reforms* (January 1994) (available on the LC MARVEL gopher: telnet to *marvel.loc.gov* and login as *gopher*).

8. American Library Association. Telecommunications and Information Infrastructure Policy Forum. *Principles for the Development of the National Information Infrastructure. [Working Draft]* (Chicago, IL, ALA, 1993)

9. American Library Association. Telecommunications and Information Infrastructure Policy Forum. *Telecommunications and Information Infrastructure Policy Forum Proceedings: Principles for the Development of the National Information Infrastructure, September 8-10, 1993* (Chicago, IL, ALA, 1993).

10. Office of Management and Budget, "Management of Federal Information Resources (OMB Circular No. A-130)," 58 *Federal Register* 36068-36086 (July 2, 1993).

11. Ibid, 36083.

12. *From Red Tape to Results: Creating a Government that Works Better and Costs Less. Report of the National Performance Review* (Washington, D. C., GPO, 1993).

13. *Milestone 5. Reinventing Support Services. National Performance Review, Accompanying Report XX* (July 29, 1993) Unpublished.

14. *Less Access to Less Information by and about the U.S. Government* (Semi-annual) Washington, D.C., American Library Association Washington Office, 1981-).

15. Wilson, David. L. "Scholars Say Financial Barriers Limit Electronic Access to Federal Data," *Chronicle of Higher Education* (February 17, 1993): A17.

16. National Technical Information Service, "Transfer by Federal Agencies of Scientific, Technical and Engineering Information to the National Technical Information Service . . . Final Rule," 59 *Federal Register* 6-12 (January 3, 1994).

17. Ibid, 12.

18. Office of Management and Budget, *Government Information Locator Service (GILS). Draft. Report to the Information Infrastructure Task Force* (Washington, D.C.: OMB, January 22, 1994).

19. Office of Management and Budget, "Management of Federal Information Resources," 36083.

20. *Alternatives for Restructuring the Depository Library Program: a Report to the Superintendent of Documents and the Public Printer from the Depository Library Council* (Washington, D.C.: Depository Library Council, September 1993).

21. Dupont Circle Draft Discussion Documents, and the *Dupont Circle Reporter* are available on the LC MARVEL gopher (telnet to *marvel.loc.gov* and login as *gopher*).

22. "Reinventing Access to Federal Government Information; Report of the Conference on the Future of Federal Government Information, Chicago, IL, October 29-31, 1993," *Documents to the People* 21 (December 1993): 234-246.

OTHER SOURCES OF INFORMATION

ALAWON (ISSN 1069-7799), is an irregular publication of the American Library Association Washington Office, 110 Maryland Avenue, N.E., Washington D.C., 20002-5675. *ALAWON* is one of the best ways to keep informed about federal library and information policy and developments. *ALAWON* is available free of charge in electronic form. To subscribe, send the message SUBSCRIBE ALAWON [YOUR NAME] to the following address *listserv@uicvm* (Bitnet) or *listserv@uicvm.uic.edu*. A printed publication, *ALA Washington Newsletter*, is available by subscription from the ALA Washington Office.

Electronic Public Information Newsletter. Contact Editor James McDonough at *epin@access.digex.net* or (301) 365-3621.

GOVDOC-L is an online discussion list on government information issues. To subscribe, send the message SUBSCRIBE GOVDOC-L [YOUR NAME] to the listserv address: *listserv@psuvm* (Bitnet) or *listserv@psuvm.psu.edu* (Internet).

Information Infrastructure Project, Kennedy School of Government, *Information Infrastructure Sourcebook.* Cambridge: Harvard University, 1993).

Information Infrastructure Task Force Bulletin Board. Internet access: Gopher to *iitf.doc.gov* or telnet to *iitf.doc.gov* and login as *gopher.*

White House Electronic Publications and Public Access Email; Frequently Asked Questions (Updated January 29, 1994). Available in many Internet locations, including the LC MARVEL gopher listed above.

Fee-Based Services
and the Future of Libraries

Stephen Coffman

It doesn't take a clairvoyant to see that libraries are in trouble. In California, the County of Los Angeles Public Library, once the largest public library in the country, suffered a budget cut of over 40% in the 1992/1993 fiscal year, and was forced to layoff over 300 full- and part-time staff, and significantly reduce hours in all of its 82 branches. As of this writing, there was no money for materials whatsoever.

Alameda County Library was hit with a 52.5% cut and has slashed its material budget by 65%, cut open hours at most branches to 18 per week, and instituted new fees for reserves and interlibrary loan. In Fresno, California, they have put spare change cans out at the circulation and reference desks in an effort to make up for some of the massive budget cuts they have suffered. Libraries in San Benito County, California and Red Bluff, California have closed altogether, and patrons of the Merced County, California system had been told to return all books and materials by December 8, 1993, when the library would be shutting its doors for good after the voters failed to approve a new tax that would have supported it.

Stephen Coffman is Director of FYI, The Professional Research and Rapid Information Delivery Service of the Los Angeles County Public Library, Los Angeles, CA. He is also past chair of Fee-Based Information Service Centers in Academic Libraries (F.I.S.C.A.L.), an ALA/ACRL Discussion Group.

[Haworth co-indexing entry note]: "Fee-Based Services and the Future of Libraries." Coffman, Stephen. Co-published simultaneously in *Journal of Library Administration* (The Haworth Press, Inc.) Vol. 20, Nos. 3/4, 1995, pp. 167-186; and: *The Future of Information Services* (ed: Virginia Steel, and C. Brigid Welch) The Haworth Press, Inc., 1995, pp. 167-186. Multiple copies of this article/chapter may be purchased from The Haworth Document Delivery Center [1-800-3-HAWORTH; 9:00 a.m. - 5:00 p.m. (EST)].

California is a particularly bleak example because of the serious structural problems in the state's economy, and because disgruntled taxpayers have made it extraordinarily difficult to pass new revenue measures. However, things don't look good anywhere in the nation. During the past few years libraries across the country have experienced major budget cuts, staff layoffs, and severe reductions or even outright elimination of materials budgets. While the January 1993 *Library Journal* Budget Survey[1] indicates that things might have moderated a little as the economy begins to recover, the overall picture is still pretty grim.

Worst of all, voters across the country have shown an increasing reluctance to pass library bonds or revenue measures of any sort. After the general failure of library referenda in the November 1990 elections, Virginia's Deputy State Librarian Nolan T. Yellich noted that "the general public is not interested in raising taxes or authorizing activity at the local and state levels that would further reduce levels of personal income, even at the expense of reductions and/or eliminations of vital public services, including those provided by libraries."[2] And in "Hitting the Fiscal Wall," Ted Gaebler, co-author of the recent best-seller *Reinventing Government*, notes that government expenditures as a percentage of GNP have been declining in both Europe and America for a number of years, and cautions governments about treating the current fiscal down turn as a short-term problem:

> It is not just something that's due to the administration in Washington, or even the recession. It is a sea change in people's willingness to spend money on government . . . The bottom line is that it is impossible for anybody in government—at the state, county, or city level—to solve the equation of providing services with tax dollars . . . The feds aren't going to provide it, and the states aren't going to provide it. State and local governments are going to have to become more self-sufficient and therefore more entrepreneurial.[3]

Considering that nearly 90% of public library revenues currently come from state and local government sources, these trends could have a devastating impact on the financial health of those institutions that fail to heed Gaebler's warnings.

THE ACADEMICS ALSO FACE PROBLEMS

Nor are academic libraries exempt from fiscal woes. Funding at many of the state-supported institutions was affected by the same constraints affecting public libraries. More broadly, the recent Mellon Report on the University Library and Scholarly Communications indicated that ever since the early 1970s major research libraries have been fighting a losing battle in their efforts to maintain comprehensive collections of scholarly literature. During the period 1970-1982 the number of titles added by the group of 24 major research libraries studied in the Mellon Report decreased at an average rate of − 1.4 percent per year, while the total number of titles published worldwide grew at an average rate of +2.0 percent per year.[4] Not only that, but university spending on libraries has declined from a high of 3.8% of general and educational expenses in 1979 to the 3.1% it comprises today. So, even though the Mellon Report showed that total library expenditures grew at an average rate of 9.2 percent per year between 1963-1991, the output of scholarly literature and the cost of purchasing and housing that literature was growing faster still, so that no matter how fast library budgets increased, the "behinder they got."

CLOSING OF LIBRARY SCHOOLS

However, the most damning evidence of the serious and long-term nature of the problems facing libraries and librarians, is the continued closing of library schools at public and private institutions around the country over the past few years. Since 1978, the profession has lost over 20% of accredited MLS programs, including the oldest and most venerable of them at Columbia University, and we are on the verge of losing a number of others, including the programs at both UC Berkeley and UCLA. The reasons cited are many, including the lack of significant scholarly research by library school faculty, the meager financial contributions of alumni, and the low salaries of librarians as compared with the high cost of graduate education. But the overall problem was probably best summed up by Jonathan Cole in his "Report to the Provost on the School of

Library Science at Columbia" in which he cited the university's need to "reduce our investment in programs of marginal quality and limited potential."[5]

All of which is clear evidence of a fundamental and deep-seated lack of confidence in the future of libraries and of those who would run them, by the academic establishment and, by extension, the society that they represent. And while some of the perennial optimists in the profession may think our current difficulties are only a temporary setback on the road to a brighter future, those who fund us, and those who have been closing the library schools obviously see these troubles as the "writing on the wall."

INCREASING COMPETITION

While libraries have been closing or struggling to stay afloat, enterprising companies have begun to discover the commercial potential of what we do, and are competing with us to sell much of the same information the public has declined to pay for through taxes.

Many of the commercial online services that were originally developed to help facilitate the research in libraries are beginning to look and act more and more like libraries themselves all the time. This is especially true as cost of computer storage has declined, and full text begins to take the place of bare bones bibliographic databases.

For example, the opening menu for the Dow Jones News Retrieval Service now looks very much like a directory you might find in the foyer of a well-stocked corporate library with sections for Company News and Information, Industry News, International News and Information, Newspapers, Magazines, Trade Publications and Newsletters, and Quotes, Market Data and Analysis. All of this information is available full-text to anyone with a subscription at the touch of a few keys. However, unlike most corporate libraries, the material in Dow Jones is always up-to-date, always on the shelf, available 18 hours per day from almost anywhere in the world, and you don't have to worry about anybody "shushing you" while you are using it.

But Dow Jones is not alone in this field. Services such as Compuserve, America Online, Prodigy and others are offering similar services to the general public which is purchasing computers and modems at ever-increasing rates. The American Chemical Society and others are developing systems that are bringing convenience and accessibility of the electronic library directly to scholarly researchers.

Nor are these systems designed expressly for the "information elite" as many have claimed. Prices for the services directed at the general public, such as Prodigy and Compuserve, are less than the cost of a subscription to cable television, and many feature flat-rate unlimited usage. Prices for specialized services such as Dow Jones are higher, but have been declining as these services have been able to reach larger markets of end-users. And it is not entirely out of the question that we might someday see some commercial online services supported entirely by advertising revenues, in much the same way as commercial television is funded now.

If all of this is not disturbing enough, right now, companies like ATT and TCI, Time Warner and others, companies with billions of dollars at their disposal, are racing to develop the infrastructure for a new "Information Superhighway" which will be able to bring articles, books, videos, newspapers, games, shopping, and all manner of education, information and entertainment services direct to your television set. A development which promises to make Dow Jones and all of the other services we are familiar with today look like very small potatoes indeed. And with all the hype surrounding the "Superhighway" you wonder why anyone would bother going down to their local library, when ATT and others are promising to pipe everything we want right into our livingrooms.

REINVENTING LIBRARIES–
HOW CAN FEE-BASED SERVICES HELP

The evidence shows that the traditional library that we have known and loved over the years is today a very beleaguered institution. It is threatened by a decline in public funding, it is unable to keep up with the output of published literature, and it is being challenged by an ever growing number of commercial online services and other information distribution systems which promise to do everything the library does, but better, faster, cheaper and in the privacy of your own home. No institution could undergo such radical changes in its environment and remain unscathed. And there is no doubt that, if the library is to survive at all, it will come out a rather different institution than that we know today. As W. David Penniman has noted in his article on "Shaping the Future:"

> To remain as we are–that is, to remain vital–we must change. If we do not change, we won't remain vital.[6]

The real question, then, is not whether we shall change, but how? What will we become? What will libraries look like? What will librarians be doing, if we do manage to survive and reinvent ourselves?

Only a fool would pretend to have all the answers to these questions, and the best any of us can do at this point is to speculate and extrapolate based upon what we know. The answers, if there are to be any, are likely to come from many sources. One of the more promising avenues for such exploration is to see how fee-based information services might help us to develop more viable and sustainable models of library service to meet the demands of our changing environment, and to speculate on the role they might play in reinventing libraries.

Fees in libraries are not a recent phenomenon. Most libraries have been charging their patrons for a variety of things, for years. The most common is the "fine" for an overdue book, but there are also charges for photocopying, and other reprographic services, and many also charge for reserves, ILL, meeting rooms, and other incidental services not considered central to a library's main mission.

However, it is only in recent years–since the development of online searching and the proliferation of the fax machine–that some libraries have begun to take the concept of fee-for-service a little farther and to establish full-fledged fee-based information services to handle the increasing demand for research and document delivery. According to the most recent edition of the FISCAL Directory of Fee-Based Research and Document Supply Services, there are now over 400 fee-based services in libraries around the world.[7]

Some of these services have been in business for quite awhile. The services at Rice University, Georgia Tech, and the University of

Minnesota and Minnesota Public Libraries, for example, have been around for over 20 years. However, most have been established within the last 5-10 years, and the past few years have seen a particularly rapid growth of fee-based document delivery services– largely because there has been a big demand for this service as fax machines have become broadly distributed, and because document delivery services are not difficult to set-up or expensive to operate.

Growth among full-service fee-based services–those that offer comprehensive research and document delivery services–has been slower. This is primarily due to the fact that such services are very difficult and expensive to set-up and operate, and because no library has yet been able to demonstrate that they have truly recovered their costs. Which brings us to the most critical point about the current status of fee-based services in libraries, and that is that, so far, none of them has proved to be a resounding financial success. In her recent article for *Library Journal*, "Fee-Based Services: Are They Worth It," Wendy Smith concludes that it is difficult to tell whether fee-based services are actually making any money, but that "It is clear that fees are not a quick fix for a library's financial problems."[8] It is difficult to get those who operate services to speak for the record, but it is doubtful that even the largest services have revenues of more than $400,000 gross and more are probably around the $200,000 range. When you figure in direct expenses, arcane overhead rates, peculiar institutional cost-accounting systems and high salary and benefit rates, as Wendy Smith said, it is difficult to tell what percentage of that gross, if any, is actually profit. However, it is certainly clear that most services are doing little better than covering costs, and they have not proved a significant source of additional revenue for libraries. Indeed, there are a number of cases where established fee-based services have been closed down after the library came to the conclusion that they were actually a drain on the institution.

For the purposes of this article, then, the question, clearly, is not so much what fee-based services are now, because so far the evidence indicates that their impact on overall library service has been marginal, at best. Rather the question is what they might be, and how the ideas and concepts that underlie and inform these fledgling services may help define new models for libraries in the future.

SUPPLEMENTING BASIC SERVICES

First and foremost, fee-based services can broaden the range and types of services and products libraries can offer to their patrons; products and services which would otherwise not be available at any price.

A simple example of this is Charles Robinson's video collection at Baltimore Public. When the budget authorities balked at spending money on videos, Robinson borrowed money from the general acquisitions budget and started a video rental service which now pays for itself and contributes over $350,000 per year to the general acquisitions budget. Many would argue that videos ought to be free, but in Baltimore the choice was between video rentals or no videos at all, so fees made it possible for the library to offer a service which otherwise would not have been available.[9]

The same rationale is behind many of the fee-based document delivery services libraries are establishing. With the proliferation of fax machines in recent years, libraries have been experiencing an increasing demand to fax copies of articles and other materials directly to patron's homes and offices. It costs a lot of money to pull an article, photocopy it, and have somebody stand and watch it as it goes out over the fax machine. So libraries are faced with a choice: they either offer the service and charge a fee to cover their costs, or they don't offer the service at all. There are a few libraries that fax for free out of their general operating budgets, but that just means that there is less money available for basic services, and most libraries end up strictly rationing such free fax services to keep demand in check (no more than two articles at time, no faxing out of area, etc.). Moreover, offering fax services at no charge puts the library in the rather peculiar position of providing staff time, photocopy charges and telecommunications costs for free to patrons who are wealthy enough to own fax machines, while charging the patron who is unfortunate enough to have to come to the library and do his own work, .15-.25 per page to photocopy the same material at the self-service machine.

It is the same situation with the many academic libraries which have established fee-based services to help them provide services to off-campus businesses, professionals and other "non-primary" clientele. In these cases, it is often a choice between setting up a fee-based service to handle the demand from off-campus users, or closing their doors to them all together. Academic libraries are funded to develop collections and provide basic services to the faculty, students and others in the academic community. When they are forced to divert resources to serve the general public, their primary mission suffers. Yet, there are many in the general public who need the resources of a good academic library. Fee-based services such as those established at the Gelman Library at George Washington University, or Rice University, or Georgia Tech, or at several hundred other campuses across the country, have allowed these libraries to expand their services to meet the needs of off-campus users, without compromising basic services to their primary clientele.

Finally, there are the full-service fee-based research and document delivery operations such as Information Researchers at the University of Illinois at Urbana-Champaign, the Inform service at Minneapolis Public, Corporate Services at New York Public, FYI at the County of Los Angeles Public Library, and several dozen others in public, academic and special libraries around the country. These services allow the library to offer their business and professional patrons personalized research and information services such as custom-produced market research reports, company profiles, extensive literature searches, expedited document delivery of almost any source from anywhere in the world and a number of other supplemental services without jeopardizing basic services to the general public.

Special research projects are very expensive undertakings, requiring hours of staff time and hundreds of dollars in direct costs. If libraries were to provide these services for free, they would quickly squander what little might be left of their operating budgets for the benefit of relatively well-off companies and individuals who are ready, willing and able to pay for the special services they need. On the other hand, libraries that do not offer such services at all may be ignoring a clearly demonstrated information need on the part of some of its best customers.

Fee-based services allow libraries to offer their customers a choice: come in and do your own research or we will do it for you, come in and photocopy your own article or we will deliver it to you. Come and use our basic services for free, or you can take advantage of our many specialized, supplemental services for a fee, but one way or the other, you can count on us to get you the information you need.

But fee-based services don't have to be limited to videos, document delivery and research services, or to serving off-campus clientele. Today libraries are beginning to experiment with a variety of new and non-traditional fee-based products and services. The County of Los Angeles operates Audio Express, a fee-based audio-books-by-mail program targeted at wealthy commuters. Some libraries are offering their patrons business and consumer mailing lists, others are experimenting with fee-based criss-cross services, as well as trademark and patent search services, and a number of other specialized products and services. In her review for *Library Journal* of fee-based services, Wendy Smith mentions that one of the most frequently floated proposals for new fee-based services is "books-by-mail for yuppie parents . . . a plan that would offer monthly packages of books, custom-selected by age and interest, which could later be mailed back by those too busy to visit the library."[10] One law library is planning to sell a selection of self-help legal texts on divorce and other popular subjects for patrons who want their own copies to keep. The publisher is providing the titles on consignment, and the library receives the standard trade discounts. And a number of libraries–including such venerable institutions as the Library of Congress and New York Public, have long maintained retail gift stores which sell a variety of merchandise including books. Of course, many libraries have recently begun to offer access to the new fee-based document delivery systems offered by CARL Uncover, OCLC, and others in an effort to increase the range of document delivery options available to their patrons. And in a move which would begin to merge the functions of library and bookstore, there is even a plan afoot which would allow library patrons to purchase a copy of any book in print for next day delivery to their own doorstep, with the library receiving a percentage on each sale.[11]

Of course, not everyone will agree that all of the offerings described here are clearly fee-based products or services. Obviously, many libraries do not charge for videos, there are some libraries which offer free local fax service, and some academic libraries allow off-campus patrons to use their collections without charge. And that's as it should be; for each library and each institution will have to draw the line between free and fee-based services for itself depending on its own financial situation, its own priorities and the needs of its patrons. But once that decision is made and the line has been drawn, no matter where it has been drawn–fee-based services permit libraries to step over the line–to supplement their basic free services to offer their patrons a much broader choice of information products and services than would otherwise be possible.

ESTABLISHING A MARKETPLACE FOR LIBRARY SERVICES

Fee-based services are also helping to bring the discipline and efficiencies of the marketplace to the business that libraries do with each other.

Libraries have traditionally relied on the interlibrary loan system to get access to information in each others' collections. Interlibrary loan arrangements were originally based on some notion of the common good or "reciprocity" so that supplying libraries generally loaned materials to requesting libraries at little or no charge on the assumption that the requesting library would extend the same courtesy to them should the occasion arise. While this approach may look good in theory, in practice it has lead to a wasteful and inefficient system, overburdened with arcane protocols and procedures guaranteed to deter all but the most stalwart of patrons. Those who do manage to place a request often must wait six to eight weeks before their material arrives, even if it is only coming from a library across town. Needless to say, most libraries have done little to promote the interlibrary loan (when was the last time you saw a sign on the reference desk saying "Ask me about our ILL service!"?), and although usage has shown a marked increase in the past few years, it is not nearly what it could be if it really were designed to serve patrons' needs. On top of all that, the service is expensive; a recent cost study by the Association of Research Libraries showed that the average cost of an ILL transaction was $29.55, and while that may not seem like an extraordinary amount of money, in 1991-1992 ARL libraries alone spent over 71 million dollars on interlibrary loan, and if all libraries were figured in, the number would probably reach into the billions.

Contrast that with the market-based document delivery services offered by commercial document suppliers and fee-based services. In the first place customer satisfaction is key, as Lee Anne George notes in her recent article "Fee-Based Information Services and Document Delivery:"

> Because fee-based services are supported totally, or in large part, by the fees charged by users, user satisfaction is their primary goal. If users aren't satisfied, they won't come back. If users don't come, the service can't recover its costs. A service that doesn't recover its costs will cease to exist. The motivation to meet client demands is obviously high.[13]

Secondly, fee-based services treat document delivery as a strictly commercial transaction. There are no protocols or procedures, there are no standards or manuals. Supplying libraries sell documents from their collections at full cost, and requesting libraries are free to get the material from who ever can give them the best deal, without regard to whether any particular supplier happens to be a net lender or a net borrower or any other criteria. Delivery times are measured in hours instead of weeks, and costs are typically half or less what ARL libraries are paying for interlibrary loan. Not only that, but competition between document suppliers provides a continual incentive for services to provide better, quicker, and cheaper document services, or see their customers drained off to someone else who will.

The fee-based document delivery model only requires that the price of obtaining information from outside the local collection should reflect the full cost of the transaction–the cost to the supplying library, and the cost to the requesting library.

It says nothing about who should pay the cost of that transaction . . . that's up to the individual library and to the patron. Some particularly well-endowed academic libraries may want to cover anything their faculty might request, just as they now go out and buy any book the faculty asks for. Other libraries will probably subsidize access to particular titles and pass along the full costs to the patrons on others, and of course, patrons–or rather individuals– would also be free to order any material they wanted from any supplier they wanted without the aide of a library at all, provided they were willing to pay the price.

But libraries can buy more than copies from one another, they can also purchase services.

No single library can claim to be proficient in all subjects, or to provide all the services its patrons need with equal efficiency. Just as the new "virtual corporations" outsource services and functions which cannot be performed efficiently in house, libraries can take advantage of the specialized services, resources and expertise at other institutions to help improve the quality and efficiency of their own operations.

Fee-based services provide the mechanism which allows libraries to take advantage of the specialized resources and expertise available at other institutions. Buying reference or research services from other libraries may not be as simple as purchasing a copy of an article or requesting a book loan, still it can be done, as those of us who run fee-based services are demonstrating everyday.

For example, since August 1993, FYI and the County of Los Angeles Public Library have been purchasing research and document delivery services from the Information Researchers service at University of Illinois at Urbana-Champaign. FYI projects which cannot be handled effectively in-house are subcontracted with Information Researchers. Staff at Information Researchers negotiate the projects directly with FYI customers, using FYI rates. Projects are then completed and delivered to the customer from Illinois under a joint FYI/Information Researchers letterhead. Likewise, document delivery requests which cannot be supplied by FYI are faxed to Urbana, which fills them at FYI rates. The arrangement has proved highly beneficial to all parties in the transaction: FYI customers get access to the resources and expertise at one of the largest academic institutions in the country at no additional charge; FYI is able to provide its customers with a much broader range of services much more efficiently than was possible with the County resources alone; and Information Researchers gets access to a huge new market in Southern California.

But this is only the beginning of what's possible if library services were available for purchase in the marketplace.

Although it hasn't happened yet, there is no reason why a library with strong reference services in a particular subject area couldn't make those services available on a subscription basis to libraries that could not afford to develop their own services in-house. How about a business reference service provided by one of the business specialty centers at a major urban public library, or medical reference services by the National Library of Medicine, or a subscription legal reference service provided by a major law library. Subscribing libraries would purchase these services on behalf of their patrons just as they would any book or periodical and there need be no charge to the patrons themselves. All of this may sound a bit far-fetched, but it is a only a logical extension of existing relationships such as that between FYI and Information Researchers; improvements in video, telecommunications and other remote access technologies are making such arrangements more practical everyday.

The point here is that whether you are talking about document delivery, or research, or reference services, there is no reason libraries should be constrained to producing everything in house, especially when it is often more efficient to buy what we need outside. Fee-based services provide the mechanism and the competitive marketplace which will help develop and sustain commerce between libraries, and commerce between libraries means better and more efficient information services for everyone.

A POTENTIAL SOURCE OF REVENUE

Finally, fee-based services represent a potential new source of revenue for libraries. Potential, because, although none of them have yet generated much in the way of profits for their libraries, they do have the basic elements necessary to do so: They sell products and services and they collect money from customers. All we have to do is find ways of reducing their costs or increasing their sales, so that there is some left over for the library when the transaction is complete.

And profitability may not be as difficult to attain as some have suggested. There are commercial document delivery and research services offering the same services as we do, and making money at it, and with far less in the way of resources than what we have to offer. All we have to do is to take a few pages out of their books and learn to manage these services like the businesses they really are.

Or better yet, why not invite the commercial services to do it for us. Libraries have the resources: millions upon millions of books, millions of periodical subscriptions, huge, well-organized and well-maintained collections of material available no where else. And we have the market: everyday, hundreds of thousands of people walk through our doors looking for information. They have the business expertise and the cost structure it takes to succeed in this field. Why not bring the two of them together and offer our research and document delivery services as a concession to commercial vendors in exchange for a percentage of the revenue they generated? For example, a library that wanted to offer its patrons fee-based research services could set up a concession with a private information brokerage, just as airports, parks, museums and other public institutions have with the restaurants, gift stores and other retail businesses which operate within their facilities. The information brokerage would lease facilities within the library where they would have ready access to the library resources and to the huge market of potential customers among library patrons and, in exchange, they would pay the library rent on the space, plus a percentage of their gross revenues.

One way or the other, if libraries can find a way to make these services more profitable, then the revenues they generate can be used to support basic library services.

There are some who feel that libraries (at least public libraries) should be entirely publicly funded, and that any attempt to develop other sources of revenue will jeopardize what funding we now have. But such arguments are short-sighted. In the first place, if we really took them at face value, we should stop all efforts to develop sources of outside funding of any type including endowments, contributions, grants, and anything else that didn't come directly from the taxpayers pocket, because each of these, like fee-based services, represents a potential source of outside income to the library, and so could threaten public funds.

Second and most importantly, many public institutions that offer services similar to ours such as museums, performing arts centers, parks, monuments and other cultural and recreational facilities are partially funded by commercial revenues they generate. What about such institutions as the Smithsonian and the Metropolitan Museum of Art which generate millions of dollars every year from product sales through their catalogs and retail stores? What about Los Angeles County Parks and Recreation where over 30% of their revenues come from commercial operations and concessions in the public parks? What about the public institutions of higher education which support many of our finest libraries? They have developed highly diversified funding sources, including tuition, grants, endowments, sponsored research, as well as a wide array of commercial enterprises ranging from football programs to hospitals to operating airports. And what of the thousands of other museums, orchestras, arboretums, parks, beaches, and other cultural and recreational institutions who have seen that the glory days of public largesse are over, and that if they and their institutions are going to survive, they are going to have to wean themselves from exclusive dependence on the public till, and diversify their sources of support.

Perhaps its time that the library community woke up and "got a clue." We are hardly exempt from funding cuts, as the experience in California proves. If we would survive, we owe it to our patrons and we owe it to ourselves to do a better job exploiting all of our resources, and that includes potential revenues from fee-based services and other entrepreneurial activities.

A NEW MODEL OF LIBRARY SERVICE

If you take the fundamental properties of fee-based services outlined above, and fully develop and exploit them, it is possible to put together a new model of library service that might look something like this.

First, you would continue to have a basic core of services which were funded by the community, just as they are today. These would include: access to the local collections and some outside collections, borrowing books and materials, basic reference and information services, and children's story times, author talks and all of the other amenities we associate with traditional library service. Basic services would also be defined by the level of service provided . . . using material in the library and making a photocopy would be free, but if you wanted us to fax it to you, you would have to pay. Patrons would be welcome to do their own research with the able assistance of the reference staff, but if you wanted us to do it, write it up and deliver it to you, it would cost you extra. Standard services would be free, but you would pay extra for extraordinary services, such as rush services, reserve services or maybe even rental of current best selling books and videos, just as many libraries are doing today. The function of this portion of the library would be the same as it is today: to provide for the basic information needs of its patrons, to help insure a better informed citizenry, to help support formal educational programs, and to maintain and preserve the record of our civilization.

In addition to these basic services, the library would offer a whole range of supplementary products and services which were funded through purchase by individual patrons. These might include: personalized research, document delivery and perhaps even clerical support services, purchase of books, articles, and other material, and a broad range of other information products, limited only by the patron's interests. Fee-based services would also be defined by level of service: if you wanted an article delivered to your home or office, you would pay for it, but you could come down to the library and use the same material for free. If you wanted your research done for you or you wanted to purchase it pre-packaged, there would be a charge; if you wanted to do it yourself, it would be free. The purpose of this portion of the library would be to assure the patron of the availability of a broad range of information products and services, and that access to information was not limited solely to what community funding would support.

The line between basic free services and those funded by private purchase would depend on the community and the level of service it was willing to tax itself to support . . . just as it does today. The only difference here is that the definition of library service no longer has to be limited to whatever the community is willing to fund, because whatever the community is unwilling to support, could be provided on a fee-basis. In fact, the only real limit to the information the library could provide in this model would be the market itself. As long as there were sufficient numbers of people who wanted to buy a particular product or service, the library would provide it. If there were not sufficient demand, the library simply would not offer it.

This model also envisions a library which is a much more active participant in the commercial field. It wouldn't just limit itself to buying books and materials as it does today, it could go to the information marketplace established between libraries, and buy access to outside collections, or reference services, or other information products, or anything else it needed to meet its users needs, and which it could not produce as efficiently or as inexpensively itself.

Of course, the marketplace would also permit the library to sell its wares to others. This might include access to its collections to other libraries or outside users, access to outside collections to its own users, and of course it would also be free to sell specialized reference and other services or information products it might have developed for its own markets to other libraries and customers as well.

Finally, this library would be in much better financial health than the institutions we know today. Its overall costs of operations should be lower because it would be free to purchase services which it is now forced to provide in-house, in an open and competitive marketplace. Meanwhile, it could take in revenues from the sales of its own products and services, or perhaps from a commercial concession leasing space in its facilities. These new sources of revenue would help diversify the library funding base and reduce its current and very dangerous dependence on tax revenues alone.

The average library patron would continue to have access to whatever level of library service the community was willing to support for free, just as they do today. The only difference would be that under this model, if they wanted something badly enough to spend some of their money on it, they would now have access to a variety of additional information products and services which today are simply not available to them at any price.

The underlying assumption of the above model is that the fundamental function of the library ... any library ... is to bring a broad selection of information services and products together in one place, regardless of how they are paid for, or who pays for them. Just as supermarkets bring most of the food and other daily necessities together in one place; just as malls have allowed us to do much of our retail shopping at one site; and just as our universities bring together many different education programs on one campus; so, too, does it make sense for libraries to bring together many of the different types and kinds of information under one roof. That's an essential function of a library, and our customers want it, and there is no doubt that somebody will provide it for them, if we are unwilling.

In that sense, it is possible to be optimistic about the future of libraries. They will survive because they are needed, and if we are unable to fill that need, then there are many others who are more than willing to take our places. The only real question, then, is are we going to be the ones behind the desk providing these services, or are we ready to cede the entire field to the likes of Dow Jones or ATT or TCI or Time Warner? And the answer will depend in large part on our ability to exploit the potential of fee-based information services to give our customers more of what they really want.

NOTES

1. "LJ's Third Annual Budget Report: PLs Struggle to Make Ends Meet." *Library Journal.* January 1993 pp. 16-36.

2. Quinn, Judy and Michael Rogers. "The Fiscal Fate of the States, 1990" in the *Library and Book Trade Almanac.* 36th ed. New Providence, New Jersey, R.R. Bowker, 1991. p. 3.

3. Gaebler, Ted. "Hitting the Fiscal Wall" *Government Technology.* February 1993, v.6 n.2. pp. 1,58.

4. *University Libraries and Scholarly Communication.* Washington D.C., Association of Research Libraries, 1992. p. xx.

5. "Report to the Provost on the School of Library Science at Columbia" April 13, 1990. p. 2.

6. Penniman, W. David. "Shaping the Future." *Library Journal* October 15, 1992. p. 41.

7. *Fiscal Directory of Fee-Based Research and Document Supply Services.* 4th ed. Chicago, American Library Association, 1993.

8. Smith, Wendy. "Fee-Based Services: Are They Worth It." *Library Journal.* June 15, 1993. p. 43.

9. ibid., p. 42.

10. ibid., p. 42.

11. This is just one of several components of the Librarium Project, currently under design by Bookworm Express, Inc., Claremont, CA.

12. "The Cost of Interlibrary Loan" *ARL: A Bi-monthly Newsletter of Research Library Issues and Actions.* #166, January 1993. p. 1.

13. George, Lee Anne. "Fee-Based Information Systems and Document Delivery. *Wilson Library Bulletin.* February 1993. p. 41.

The Role of Information Professional in Selecting Vendor Services

George R. Plosker
Linnea J. Christiani

Fourteen years ago a paper, "Management of Vendor Services: How to Choose an Online Vendor," that was written by one of the co-authors of this paper and former DIALOG President Roger Summit, stated ". . . virtually all libraries are thinking of enhancing reference services with online resources.[1] Today, with the "Virtual Library" upon us, it is clear that electronic access to information resources is becoming a fact of life for all libraries and information centers.

The aim of this paper is to consider the role of information professionals in selecting vendor services within the context of the theme "the future of information services."

It is our intent to review the many options that today's information professional has in terms of selection of vendor services and to provide both historical context and a forecast for key factors in such

---

George R. Plosker is Senior Manager of Client Services, and Linnea J. Christiani is Senior Manager of Licensing and Distribution for Information Access Company, Foster City, CA. Mr. Plosker has an MA in Librarianship from San Jose State University. Ms. Christiani has an MLIS from the University of California at Berkeley.

The authors wish to thank the following Information Access Company staff for their support and editing of this document: Ronnie Adams, Information Specialist, and Peter Vigil, Technical Writer.

[Haworth co-indexing entry note]: "The Role of Information Professional in Selecting Vendor Services." Plosker, George R., and Linnea J. Christiani. Co-published simultaneously in *Journal of Library Administration* (The Haworth Press, Inc.) Vol. 20, Nos. 3/4, 1995, pp. 187-196; and: *The Future of Information Services* (ed: Virginia Steel, and C. Brigid Welch) The Haworth Press, Inc., 1995, pp. 187-196. Multiple copies of this article/chapter may be purchased from The Haworth Document Delivery Center [1-800-3-HAWORTH; 9:00 a.m. - 5:00 p.m. (EST)].

decision-making. In looking over the fourteen-year-old paper mentioned above, it is obvious that the complexity of the options has increased dramatically. However, despite the many changes in technology and user expectations, many of the major decision points remain the same.

In 1980 we were trained on 300 baud TI Silent 700 Terminals; there were only a handful of online vendors; CD-ROM, E-Mail, FAX, LANs, an abundance of online full-text titles, and other familiar information technologies and capabilities of today were nonexistent.

Now the range of delivery mechanisms is exploding with change on a daily basis. Information professionals must be familiar with far more than content in striving to meet client needs. Providing a comprehensive, systematic approach to this formidable decision matrix will be the goal of this paper.

As always, the first step in evaluation of outside services is to determine what services are needed in your organization. Historically, this assessment meant what tools and reference sources would be brought into the library or information center.

In 1980, the choice was what online service would best serve the needs of the information professional. However, today we are seeing a broader point of view. In addition to the traditional intermediary role where the librarian does all of the research on behalf of the ultimate user, information professionals are also frequently examining the effectiveness of information tools for end-user searching, including selecting appropriate delivery systems and instructing others in the use of information products.

In this context, the question becomes what information products should be available to knowledge-based professionals, perhaps right at their own desks. What are the core needs of these information users? What are the more occasional needs? What is the role of the library or information center in selecting and delivering this information?

It is no longer enough to determine that a particular database or vendor meets content needs. Today's librarian must evaluate how and in what form to receive and deliver the information. Is a database used often enough to justify the cost of a CD-ROM or other site license? When are the efficiencies and improved access justified? To answer these questions, we must consider classical content-based selection, plus keep abreast of the latest in commercial and internal desk-top delivery systems.

Today it seems plausible to consider two distinct levels of needs: (1) those of the information professionals in providing intermediary service to the end-users; and (2) those of the end-users themselves. It also seems that the information industry is cognizant of this distinction, as virtually all of the traditional commercial vendors are looking to maintain their core business, while at the same time expanding to the end-user market. This is a trend that is certainly going to continue.

EVALUATING PROFESSIONAL/INTERMEDIARY SERVICES

As described in the earlier paper,[1] content remains the number one determinant of what services to choose . . . i.e., which information tools match up with subject needs.

Generally an information center will require a broad range of files, such as those provided by a database "supermarket service," combined with locally available internal files and licensed databases that are highly targeted to the industry or specialization of the organization. The online "supermarket" resources add depth and comprehensiveness to searches initiated by information professionals or end-users on local systems. This hybrid approach appears to be the future trend. However, it can also be viewed as a high-tech version of an older model, where online services supplemented the library's print collection of indexes, directories, newspapers, journals, and internal reports.

Cost is, of course, of significant concern in selecting a primary online vendor. In this area, it is critical to compare the pricing policies of the various vendors, many of which are in transition due to user demand. For what, exactly, is one being charged–time, output, initiation of a search, information units or lines of print? How easy is it to understand and control costs? How do costs relate to one's style of searching and the type of questions typically being asked?

It may also be worthwhile to investigate if volume discounts or subscription rates are available. Are such charges related to past history or the number of users at your site? How flexible are billing options? It is not always easy to determine a true net price that allows for head-to-head comparisons.

These content and cost issues have always been considered in the evaluation of information services. What is changing dramatically is the proliferation of delivery media. From the Internet to local area networks to customized Alert products, the question seems to be what new technical channels will work best for the organization.

Once the needs of the organization are identified, products and services from information vendors that may meet these requirements must be evaluated. While the choices may seem overwhelming, some classical approaches will still guide the information administrator.

In addition to traditional library sources, the information industry has generated its own body of literature, including *Online Database, Database Review, Database Searcher, Information Today,* and many more. Additional tools are listed in the bibliography that provide coverage of the offerings provided by information vendors, and evaluations of those products.

Consultation with colleagues, attending training seminars and industry conferences, especially those with exhibits offering live demonstrations, are also useful. These exhibits offer an excellent opportunity to ask the tough questions and actually observe how the product performs in a real world, demand situation. To get the most out of a visit to the Exhibit Hall, it is helpful to select the vendors or publishers in advance and come armed with specific questions or searches.

As preparation for the exhibit visit, marketing packages can be requested from each vendor under consideration. A critical review of these marketing tools, an examination of the relevant literature, and consultation with colleagues would provide objective assessment of the service.

Many of today's vendors will also allow a "test drive," i.e., a trial of the service which facilitates evaluation of the product within the local environment.

EVALUATING END-USER SERVICES

We have seen a recent proliferation of information services targeted directly at end-users. It is often the role of today's information professional to assume an advisory role in the organizational selection of end-user information tools. Library resources and capabilities must be in tune with and complementary to end-user services and sources.

Certainly traditional online remains a viable option for end-user searching, especially when one needs the broad subject coverage of a "supermarket service." However, if there is a strong focus on end-user searching, it might suggest that one or two key locally available files could answer the bulk of end-user questions.

Database producers are increasingly assuming a more direct role in information provision. Changes in user expectations, and the CD-ROM revolution, have led database publishers to offer their products in alternative media that may be more appropriate for non-professional searchers. Today the publisher may provide internal access through a "site license" which can be adapted to specific user needs. Site licensing can include CD-ROM, local tape loads, LAN distribution, and OPAC access to commercial databases.

The choice of technical delivery mechanisms should again focus on user needs. Likewise, selection of a vendor or database should be a function of the type of services a library wishes to provide or develop for its users. The trends to customize information, access, and delivery are reflected in the new options available from vendors.

Direct delivery of Alerts to E-Mail boxes, FAX output of full-text or even full-image documents, Windows-based front-ends, natural language searching with relevance ranking, and redistribution of downloaded data on local networks are available to support these needs. LAN-based search tools and passive desktop delivery systems are two of the newest options for internal information delivery.

If a library wishes to provide E-Mail or LAN access to customized Alerts or even use them as the basis for a newsletter, there are a number of issues that need to be addressed. The traditional question of database content and searchability is foremost in selecting files or a system to use because it directly affects the value of the output. One must also evaluate how easy it is to build and change an Alert profile in the system, and how much flexibility there is in the frequency. What is the basis for the price and how predictable is it? Are key publications covered, are they current and is text readily available? How difficult is it to direct results to many different mailboxes or users? How is the information displayed or presented? Does the vendor provide an interface for organizing or viewing the results?

If multiple copies will be distributed throughout the organization, there are other issues to address. Does the vendor have a redistribution program or must permission or a license be obtained from the database publisher or directly from original publishers? What are the copyright restrictions? Is the redistribution licensing fee based on the number of users, number of records distributed, or a combination of both?

If internal access is desired primarily to allow unlimited end-user searching in heavily-used databases, there are a number of options available. They include negotiating a fixed fee with a vendor, licensing a CD-ROM, or leasing and mounting tapes on an internal delivery platform. Such site licensing of data allows for not only broad, but also customized access to information. However, the type of licensing chosen should depend on the purpose and service to be provided.

The fundamental issues are access, support, and cost. Which approach provides the best search software and access to the data, and which will be easiest to maintain? Also, which delivery options are available for the desired database? If considering an online fixed-fee approach, does the vendor have an interface for novice searchers? What is the basis of the fixed fee, and how might it change on renewal? Which databases or publications are available? How many users will be served?

If the information is available on a CD-ROM, will it be used heavily enough to justify the cost? How often is it updated, and how important is currency? Is the search software appropriate for the intended users? Will multiple stations or networking be required? If so, how many users can be connected simultaneously without significantly degrading response time? Can the database also be accessed from an externally-stored system or through the library's

OPAC system to alleviate current compatibility, and access problems?

If an internal database management system is available, is it preferable to lease directly from the database publisher? Will it serve a large enough user base to justify the costs? Does the search software provide adequate access and display of bibliographic or textual databases? Do all users have access and familiarity with the software? Is there internal support for loading and updating the file and creating documentation? What kind of support would the database publisher provide? Is the file format compatible with other external or internal information sources? How often is it updated, and how are changes handled? Are backfiles available, and can they be kept if the current subscription is canceled? What is the basis for the license fee, and how might it change on renewal?

If site licensing is desired to create a customized database or to merge external and internal information, there are additional options to consider. One is to create an Alert profile and download selected records from an online vendor into an internal database. However, it should be noted that this usage generally requires special permission or an archival license from the publisher if used by more than one user.

If an archival license is available from the vendor or publisher, it is important to know if the basis for the licensing fee is the number of users with access to the database or those who actually use it. Is it based on the number of records downloaded as well as the number of users? What kind of recordkeeping is required? If a large volume of records is used, would a customized tape license or interface with an externally-loaded database be more cost effective and easier to manage?

EVALUATING VENDOR SUPPORT

In addition to content and delivery, service is an important factor to consider. The emerging complexity and competitiveness of the information marketplace has numerous advantages to the buyer of such services. The information industry has grown to understand that it must provide more than basic content, competitive pricing, and reliable technology.

Historically, vendor support included excellent documentation, effective public training classes, an informative newsletter, plus a responsive and knowledgeable toll-free customer-service hotline. The most significant change now is in the area of on-site support, including customized training for information professionals, awareness briefings to executive, department, or functional groups, specialized bibliographic instruction for end-users, and detailed follow-up as needed.

Consider the example of a large, progressive southern California technology firm. Library management recently began to request increased on-site vendor support in meeting the needs of both their information professional staff and corporate end-users. When asked about the increased interest in on-site workshops, the information center manager replied that management was requiring that all users of outside vendor services obtain "maximum value" from such suppliers. Demonstrating that one was receiving such "maximum value" from vendors was viewed as a big plus by senior management.

On-site customized training for information professionals has many advantages for the organization. Such instruction can focus on narrow subject needs of the client. It can assist the staff in remaining current with the latest in system features or enhancements to subject coverage, including new sources or files. Valuable staff time is saved, as the vendor comes to the organization instead of staff traveling to the public training site.

Another major advantage of on-site training is that confidentiality of client organization search topics is protected. In other words, searchers and trainer can consider proprietary subjects without fear that a major competitor will overhear the discussion during a public training seminar.

On-site awareness briefings to executive, department, or functional groups by vendor- or database-producer representatives serve the library particularly well. Linking these briefings to a library open-house or other similar event provides a valuable marketing tool for the information administrator. Increasing in-house knowledge of the benefits of library services is critical in today's age of shrinking budgets and resources. A better informed end-user knows when the library can be of assistance, and actively seeks out library help on projects and assignments.

Successful in-house marketing activities may also result in changing responsibilities for the information center. Not only will information specialists fulfill reference requests, but he or she may be required to assume an instructional role in end-user search efforts.

Specialized bibliographic instruction for end-users by vendor representatives can ease the burden on library staff while at the same time familiarizing end-users with important sources and tools. On-site vendor presentations can be coordinated with local bibliographic instruction, plus the vendor can be called on to co-develop, or even provide, appropriate instructional materials.

Related activities can also be supported by the vendor. Publishing an internal newsletter or inhouse electronic bulletin board? Ask for permission to reprint vendor newsletter articles or documentation paces. Introducing a new capability? Ask for training and demonstration time to support the roll-out. Evaluating a new product? Ask for a free trial.

FUTURE OUTLOOK

As new information vendors continue to emerge, the traditional ones will have to continuously evaluate their services if they are to survive and compete. This should make it an excellent buyer's market for the wise shopper and accelerate the speed of change with improved products and services.

While it is clear that libraries are facing tough times and difficult decisions, it can also be seen that today's technical developments are providing an exciting way to become closer to and better serve information users. A new relationship is emerging between user, information center, and vendor which can be the basis of improved organizational productivity and effectiveness.

NOTE

1. Plosker, George R. and Roger K. Summit, "Management of Vendor Services: How to Choose an Online Vendor." Special Libraries, Vol. 71. No. 8 (August, 1980): 354-357.

BIBLIOGRAPHY AND SELECTION AIDS

Basch, Reva. *Secrets of the Super Searchers*. Wilton, CT: Eight Bit Books, 1993.

BiblioData Fulltext Sources Online: For Periodicals, Newspapers, Newsletters & Newswires. Ed. Ruth M. Orenstein. Needham Heights, MA: Bibliodata, Biannually.

Business & Legal CD-ROMS in Print 1993: An International Guide to CD-ROM and CD-Based Multimedia Products in Business, Economics, Finance, Law, and Related Fields. Comp. Regina Rega. Ed. Norman Desmarais. Westport, CT: Meckler Publishing, 1993.

Directory of Online Databases. New York, NY: Cuadra/Elsevier, 1991.

1992 Annual. Books & Periodicals Online: The Guide to Business and Legal Information on Databases and CD-ROMS. Ed. Nuchine Nobari. New York, NY: Library Alliance, 1991.

Ulrich's International Periodicals Directory 1989-90. New York, NY: R.R. Bowker (Division of Reed Publishing (USA) Inc.), 1989.

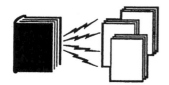

Haworth
DOCUMENT DELIVERY
SERVICE

This new service provides a single-article order form for any article from a Haworth journal.

- *Time Saving:* No running around from library to library to find a specific article.
- *Cost Effective:* All costs are kept down to a minimum.
- *Fast Delivery:* Choose from several options, including same-day FAX.
- *No Copyright Hassles:* You will be supplied by the original publisher.
- *Easy Payment:* Choose from several easy payment methods.

Open Accounts Welcome for . . .
- Library Interlibrary Loan Departments
- Library Network/Consortia Wishing to Provide Single-Article Services
- Indexing/Abstracting Services with Single Article Provision Services
- Document Provision Brokers and Freelance Information Service Providers

MAIL or *FAX* THIS ENTIRE ORDER FORM TO:

Haworth Document Delivery Service
The Haworth Press, Inc.
10 Alice Street
Binghamton, NY 13904-1580

or FAX: (607) 722-6362
or CALL: 1-800-3-HAWORTH
(1-800-342-9678; 9am-5pm EST)

PLEASE SEND ME PHOTOCOPIES OF THE FOLLOWING SINGLE ARTICLES:
1) Journal Title: _____
   Vol/Issue/Year:_____Starting & Ending Pages:_____
Article Title:_____

2) Journal Title: _____
   Vol/Issue/Year:_____Starting & Ending Pages:_____
Article Title:_____

3) Journal Title: _____
   Vol/Issue/Year:_____Starting & Ending Pages:_____
Article Title:_____

4) Journal Title: _____
   Vol/Issue/Year:_____Starting & Ending Pages:_____
Article Title:_____

(See other side for Costs and Payment Information)

COSTS: Please figure your cost to order quality copies of an article.
  1. Set-up charge per article: $8.00
                    ($8.00 × number of separate articles)   _____
  2. Photocopying charge for each article:
                              1-10 pages: $1.00   _____

                              11-19 pages: $3.00   _____

                              20-29 pages: $5.00   _____

                              30+ pages: $2.00/10 pages   _____

  3. Flexicover (optional): $2.00/article   _____
  4. Postage & Handling: US: $1.00 for the first article/
                              $.50 each additional article   _____

                          Federal Express: $25.00   _____

                          Outside US: $2.00 for first article/
                              $.50 each additional article _____

  5. Same-day FAX service: $.35 per page   _____

                              GRAND TOTAL: _____

METHOD OF PAYMENT: (please check one)
❏ Check enclosed   ❏ Please ship and bill. PO # _____
                    (sorry we can ship and bill to bookstores only! All others must pre-pay)
❏ Charge to my credit card: ❏ Visa; ❏ MasterCard; ❏ American Express;

Account Number:_____ Expiration date:_____

Signature: *X*_____

Name: _____ Institution: _____

Address: _____

          _____

City: _____ State:_____ Zip:_____

Phone Number: _____ FAX Number: _____

MAIL or *FAX* THIS ENTIRE ORDER FORM TO:

Haworth Document Delivery Service	**or FAX:** (607) 722-6362
The Haworth Press, Inc.	**or CALL:** 1-800-3-HAWORTH
10 Alice Street	(1-800-342-9678; 9am-5pm EST)
Binghamton, NY 13904-1580	